History of Britain

A Captivating Guide to Events and Facts You Should Know about the Story of England, Wales, Northern Ireland, and Scotland

Free Bonus from Captivating History
(Available for a Limited time)

Hi History Lovers!

Now you have a chance to join our exclusive history list so you can get your first history ebook for free as well as discounts and a potential to get more history books for free! Simply visit the link below to join.

Captivatinghistory.com/ebook

Also, make sure to follow us on Facebook, Twitter and Youtube by searching for Captivating History.

Table of Contents

Introduction: Back When Britannia Ruled the Waves

Today, it is almost hard to fathom that Britain was once the largest empire on the planet. We see the island of Britain, which is home to Scotland, England, and Wales, and wonder how this minuscule piece of real estate gave birth to such a juggernaut. As far as islands go, Britain is quite large; it is the ninth-largest in the world. But when compared to massive nations like China and Russia, it is easy to fall into the trap of seeing Britain as a small island that could not hold its own when faced with the threat of larger powers.

Nevertheless, for centuries, the island of Britain stood as both a lighthouse and a fortress. Since the days of the Magna Carta, Britain shined as a beacon of what a nation could achieve if only its citizenry were given the proper opportunity.

Britain brought us the plays of William Shakespeare and the first locomotives to hit the railroad tracks. In many ways, Britain was well ahead of its peers. Even so, Britain had a long history of fending off adversaries. The British Isles, which primarily consist of Britain proper and the island of Ireland (home to Ireland and Northern Ireland), were waylaid by Vikings and then subject to a Norman invasion. (As a note, the term "British Isles" is sometimes seen in a negative light due to the British Empire's dominance of Ireland. The term is still used by most scholars, which is why we have elected to use it at times in the book.)

The Anglo-Saxons were subdued in 1066 by William the Conqueror, one of the most famous men in history. However, the Norman newcomers were more likely to co-opt what they found in Britain rather than replace it with their own modes of living. William is often credited with "introducing" feudalism, but this is not entirely accurate. It has been noted that some forms of feudalism were already in existence in England prior to his arrival. However, William placed a heavier emphasis on feudalism and greatly sped up the process of making it an enshrined state institution.

Once in force, the feudal system better streamlined the control of land, allotting whole sections to various members of the elite. Most of these "elite" were William's fellow Normans who had fought alongside him to subdue England. The French-speaking Normans established castles throughout the realm, further solidifying their grip on their many landed estates.

The greatest shock of William's takeover was felt by prominent Anglo-Saxon nobility who were stripped of their land and titles. For them, the change was tremendous. But for the landless peasants, who were already landless before the invasion, the immediate impact on their daily lives was not so great. At most, they could look forward to new landlords who spoke a new language. No matter who the landed elite might have been, the general character and spirit of the British masses remained mostly the same.

Britain has long had a spirit of originality—some might even say defiance—which makes it stand on its principles without interference from others. One could say this independent streak came to prominence during Henry VIII's reign. This monarch is often lambasted for being reckless and self-centered due to his falling out with the Catholic Church over his wishes to pursue another wife and thereby produce a male heir for his throne.

But whatever you might think of this Tudor king's motives, you have to hand it to him—even when the status quo of the Roman Catholic Church refused to give him what he wanted, he was unwilling to just take no for an answer. When the Roman Catholic Church indicated that it was against their rules and regulations for him to annul his marriage, Henry VIII simply created a church of his own, the Church of England, and put himself at its head.

People might argue about whether he was right or wrong for doing so, but we can all agree that the stiff upper lip of British defiance showed itself. And it did so in countless other epochs of British history. Britain stood practically alone against the Axis Powers at the outset of World War Two after France fell, yet it stood ready to defend its way of life at all costs.

Even after British troops had been driven off the shores of Dunkirk, the bold and courageous prime minister, Winston Churchill, stood in the gap, declaring the British would fight their foes every step of the way and "never surrender."

These bold words sum up Britain's history in its entirety. From the Anglo-Saxons to Brexit, Britain has dared to be different, and the whole world has continuously stood in awe.

PART ONE: ENGLAND

Chapter 1: The Arrival of the Anglo-Saxons

"I hope for nothing in this world so ardently as once again to see that paradise called England. I long to embrace again all my old friends there."

-Cosimo III de' Medici

The Anglo-Saxons' arrival to Britain dates back to the middle of the 5th century. Just as Roman influence over Britain was coming to a close around 410, new arrivals from the European mainland known as the Anglo-Saxons began to make their presence known in large numbers. The Anglo-Saxons, which consisted of the Angles, Saxons, and Jutes, were a Germanic people group who arrived in several waves of migration. These migrants would come into direct contact (and conflict) with the Romanized Britons of southern England, which at that time is said to have been quite large.

When we say "Romanized Britons," it is important to understand these people hailed from various backgrounds and tribal groups. Among them were, of course, the Celts (at least those who chose to submit to Roman rule), Bretons, Caledonians, and Brigantes. These tribal groups were early adopters of Romanization and now found themselves in direct conflict with the Anglo-Saxon newcomers.

The Anglo-Saxons initially established their enclave in England's eastern corner—East Anglia—which is named after them. The influx of the Anglo-Saxons has been likened to a slow-moving invasion. Unlike the Roman invasion of Britain and the later Viking and Norman invasions, the Anglo-Saxons' arrival occurred in a piecemeal fashion over the centuries. According to at least one account by a monk named Gildas, there were some more overt episodes of takeover as well. Around 540, Gildas compiled a brief history of events said to have occurred in the 440s, right at the tail end of Roman influence in western Europe.

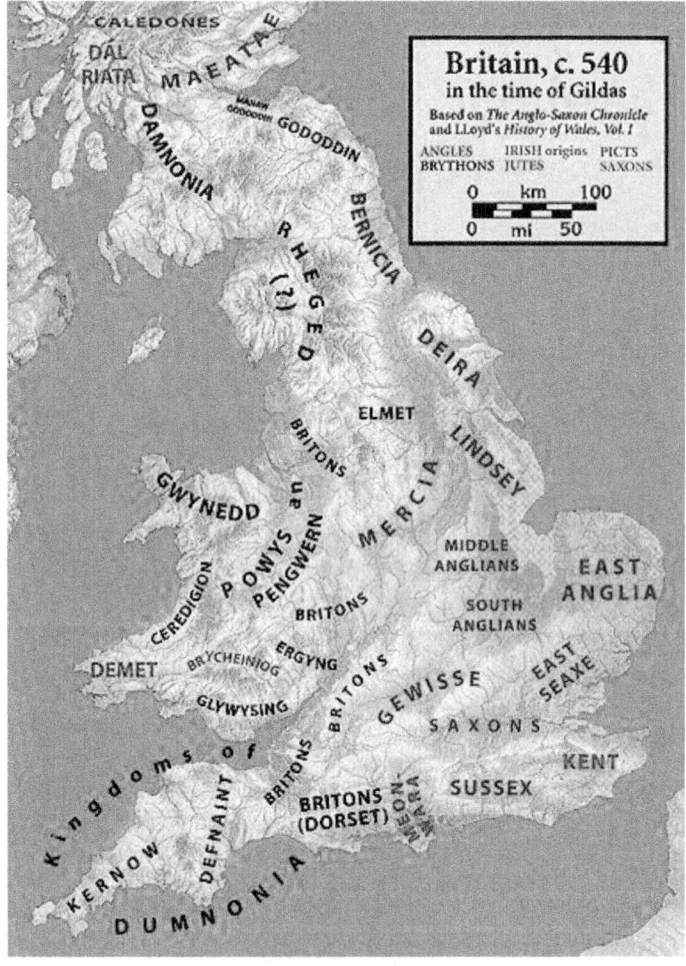

Britain in 540.

According to Gildas, in the 5th century, a British warlord named Gurthigern, better known as Vortigern, attempted to hold his own in eastern England but decided to make use of an old Roman tactic of recruiting mercenaries. This strategy led to one of the most massive influxes of Anglo-Saxons. Some question Gildas's account, saying Vortigern was not even real. However, the general consensus is that he did exist, and it is not out of the realm of possibility that he hired foreign mercenaries. And as was often the case with the Romans themselves, it would not have taken long for these hired hands to turn on their employers and attempt to seize lands outright.

As Anglo-Saxons more aggressively seized British real estate, the inhabitants of Roman Britain were pushed farther north and west in hopes of avoiding the recklessness of the Anglo-Saxons. And while the Anglo-Saxons would change the cultural landscape of Britain over time, they would also be influenced by those who had come before.

Even after the fall of the Western Roman Empire, the civil structure of Roman Britons who spoke Latin and adhered to various aspects of Roman customs would remain intact, at least for some time. Most importantly, the Latin alphabet would be adopted by the Anglo-Saxons around the year 600. The Anglo-Saxons had no written language of their own save for their symbolic runic script. This merger produced the first Anglicized literature, with Latin script, bright artistic lettering, and an Anglo-Saxon flair.

The Romans themselves had become increasingly Christian ever since Emperor Constantine's fateful Edict of Milan in 313 CE approved of Christianity. When the last Western Roman emperor, Romulus Augustus, was overthrown in 476, the Roman Catholic Church became a guiding light, with the pope taking on the guise of an ideological emperor ruling over all of the Catholics scattered throughout the former Roman Empire.

As the last remnants of Roman thought flowed into Anglo-Saxon circles, the Anglo-Saxons eventually adopted the Christian religion, as well as many aspects of Roman culture. Countless Christian missionaries played a major role in the Anglo-Saxons' conversion. They fearlessly risked life and limb to preach to warlike tribes throughout the former provinces of the Roman Empire.

As the Romanized Britons and Anglo-Saxons began to merge, their cooperation became clear. By the end of the 6th century, leading Briton and Anglo-Saxon figures were more or less in sync with each other. The Anglo-Saxon period of England created seven kingdoms: East Anglia, Essex, Sussex, Wessex, Mercia, Northumbria, and Kent. Wales was divided into the states of Gwynedd, Gwent, Dyfed, and Powys.

The Welsh maintained a strong confederation and were able to keep Anglo-Saxon encroachments at bay. But the Anglo-Saxons' inexorable push northward would eventually deprive the Welsh of their most arable farmlands, with the Anglo-Saxons moving into the Welsh Lowlands. From this point forward, the Welsh would be pigeonholed into a much more hardscrabble existence in the Welsh Highlands. Around this time, Scotland was facing some territorial changes as well.

In the late 6th century, Scotland boasted the Kingdom of Rheged, which ran from the Solway Firth all the way toward Cumbria. At this time, the northernmost reaches of Scotland were controlled by a tribal group called the Picts. Not a whole lot is known about the early history of the Picts, although we know they thrived during the British "Dark Ages." They were observed as far back as the Roman era, as the Romans appreciated their fierceness while simultaneously deriding them as barbarians. The Romans called them Picts since their warriors were covered in tattoos. "Pict" is derived from the Latin word *pictus*, which means "painted." The Romans were both awed and repulsed by these people who painted their bodies and resisted them at every turn.

By the 5th and 6th centuries, the Picts were on the rise. They had formed a confederation between several of their larger tribes. However, they were forced to become a tributary for the more powerful neighboring kingdom to their immediate south: Northumbria.

Formed in northern England and southeastern Scotland in the early 600s, Northumbria would become one of Britain's strongest, most consolidated kingdoms in the Early Middle Ages. Its starting point was just north of the Humber, an estuary, hence the name (north of the Humber). The Northumbrians descended from the Germanic tribes who had arrived in Britain during late antiquity. Northumbria is said to have been founded by a warrior king named Æthelfrith, who built up a powerful army to subdue his neighboring rivals.

Æthelfrith would ultimately perish on the battlefield in 616. He was succeeded by his brother Edwin. As king of Northumbria, Edwin, though from a pagan background, eventually turned to Christianity and used it to ideologically unify his kingdom. Northumbria officially adopted the faith in 627. Northumbria was home to Christian focal points like the majestic monastery of Lindisfarne. Here, monks laboriously compiled the Lindisfarne Gospels. This was a painstaking work of biblical scripture showcased in illuminated lettering. It would be finished sometime between 715 and 720.

A page from the Lindisfarne Gospels.

King Æthelfrith was succeeded by his son, who ruled for a few years. Oswald, another one of Æthelfrith's sons, ruled next, coming to power in 634. He greatly expanded Northumbria during his reign. His brother, King Oswiu, would succeed him and go even further by absorbing the nearby Kingdom of Mercia, making Northumbria the most impressive kingdom in Britain. However, the greatest thorn in the Northumbrians' side would remain the Picts.

After relations between the two had broken down, the Picts are said to have lured the Northumbrians into an ambush, which resulted in the disastrous Battle of Nechtansmere (also known as the Battle of Dun Nechtain) in 685. The Northumbrians were terribly defeated, even losing their king, Ecgfrith. They would never rally the strength they previously had. From here on out, the Kingdom of Northumbria would go into decline. The Picts' efforts are said to have helped ensure the northernmost regions of Britain would be too difficult for any later English ruler to conquer them.

By 750, the Picts still reigned over much of what we now call Scotland. Yet in the turbulent backdrop of the Dark Ages, the Picts would be no more. By the end of the 10th century, the Picts disappeared from the record. This in itself presents a mystery, and there is much debate as to what might have befallen the once-mighty Picts.

Some have laid the blame for the demise of the Picts on Viking incursions from Scandinavia. This theory makes a lot of sense since this would have been around when Scandinavian Vikings invaded and explored northern Britain, spreading havoc as far south as Lindisfarne Priory. Lindisfarne had one of the most memorable encounters with the Vikings, as it was the first recorded encounter of a Viking attack on Britain. In 793, the pagan invaders desecrated the monastery and ruthlessly put its monks to the sword.

Could it be then that the Vikings decimated the once-strong buffer state to the north—the kingdom of the Picts? If so, it seems the Vikings who descended from their longboats onto Britain's northernmost shores were able to do one of two things. Either they managed to catch the Picts entirely off-guard or were able to poke and prod their weakest flanks and deal devastating knockout blows, decimating the Picts' ability to fight. Neither the Romans nor the Northumbrians were ever able to do this.

As devastating as the Viking attacks were, the Viking raids proved more transitory in nature, and the Vikings did not put down permanent roots in Scotland on a large scale. In 843, a powerful leader whose name comes down to us as "Kenneth MacAlpin" sent a large force into the shattered remnants of Pict territory to establish his authority over a patchwork conglomerate, which would eventually come to be known as Scotland. Not a whole lot is known about MacAlpin's background, but he is said to have Gaelic roots.

At any rate, it is believed the remnants of the Picts were absorbed into the newcomers brought by MacAlpin. This combination of people groups resulted in the residents of Scotland that we know today.

Since the Viking threat was not yet over, it was incumbent upon MacAlpin to shore up Scotland's northern defenses (the same northern defenses that were likely vulnerable to attack from the Vikings in the first place). He amassed a large army and created a strong bulwark against future Viking raids. Due to the Picts' and Scots' common struggle against the Viking threat, some historians have theorized that the Pict survivors might have gladly accepted MacAlpin's rule as a means of survival. Siding with MacAlpin held the promise of future protection from the marauding bands of Vikings who had devastated them in previous go-arounds.

Even so, it was not long before Pictish customs and language disappeared from the scene altogether. The descendants of this historic merger would not speak Pict but rather Scottish Gaelic. They would also conform to Gaelic ideology by embracing Scottish variations of the Christian faith. This, too, was perhaps a further means of presenting a united front against the invading Vikings since the Vikings were pagans at the time. The peoples of Scandinavia would not enter into the Christian fold until much later in the game, with most not converting until after 1000, although the process began in the 900s.

The Vikings also remained a formidable thorn in the Anglo-Saxons' side. The situation came to a head in the 870s when Danish Vikings began making inroads in northwestern Britain. It took a young king from Wessex named Alfred to stand in the gap. Alfred rallied a large army and met the Vikings in an open battle near Edington. His forces were victorious and managed to stop this latest Viking onslaught in its tracks.

Upon the Vikings' defeat, their demoralized leader, Guthrum, apparently knowing that his time was up, decided to convert to Christianity and encouraged his followers to do likewise. He did this to confirm the agreement he had made with Alfred, as he wished for peace. However, this baptism made it clear to all involved that the Anglo-Saxons had triumphed both on the battlefield and on an ideological and cultural level.

Britain in 878.

Wessex became the main focal point of authority in Britain. And Alfred—later known as "Alfred the Great"—would not squander the gains he had made. Instead, he would further invest in them. With his main enemies at bay, King Alfred worked on bolstering his defenses. He wished to have not just a standing army but also a rotational system of local militias led by his immediate subordinates in the nobility class. These militias could be called upon at any time.

Alfred created a network of burhs, a series of strong fortifications spiraling out from the Wessex capital of Winchester. As a final yet incredibly important touch, Alfred revamped Wessex's naval capacity, creating an effective naval force to deter Viking incursions by sea. These modifications would prove to be useful when the Vikings launched renewed raids in the 880s and 890s.

With his northern flank secure from any further Viking incursions, by the time of his demise in 899, Alfred the Great had managed to expand his kingdom all the way to London in the south, West Mercia in the west, and Kent in the east—establishing a blueprint for what would eventually become England today. The consolidating power of Alfred served to reshape the region. As writer and historian Richard Dargie once put it, "Alfred's greatest victory lay in aligning the cause of Wessex with a wider burgeoning sense of 'Englishness.'"

Upon Alfred's passing, it was up to his son Edward to carry on the mantle. To make it official, Edward was hailed as the "King of Angles and Saxons" in 900, a title his father held later in life. King Edward was a notable champion of the realm, just like his father before him. Like Alfred the Great, he constructed mighty forts throughout the region. He was at war with the Vikings intermittently.

Edward (remembered as Edward the Elder) battled the Danes in Northumbria, always seeking to repulse them ever farther northward from the Humber, which separated Wessex from the Danelaw or Dane's Land. The culture and laws of the Danes had a tremendous impact on those around them. Many Norse words and customs would be melded with the surrounding cultures that were already in place.

But as remarkable as Edward was, in many ways, his sister, Æthelflæd, was even more remarkable. She came to prominence early on as a true fighter and defender of the realm.

As a young girl, Æthelflæd managed to foil her own attempted abduction. The Danes had conducted a raid and tried to take off with her while the princess's handlers looked on. She would have likely suffered a terrible fate if it was not for her formidable, fiery spirit to struggle. She put up such a fight against her assailants that they gave up and made a hasty retreat. Æthelflæd later married the king of Mercia (who had the very similar sounding name of Æthelred). She was absolutely adored by her subjects and would forever be known as the "Lady of the Mercians."

Edward's heir was his son Æthelstan. It is said that Æthelstan was an energetic, ambitious man with proven acumen on the field of battle. He came to the role of king ready to take Wessex from defensive to offensive campaigns. Soon, his forces were pouring into neighboring regions, expanding the borders of his kingdom until they essentially reached those associated with the borders of modern-day England. For this reason, Æthelstan is said to be the first king of England.

Under the steady hands of Æthelstan, the rest of Northumbria was brought into the domain of Wessex. He also pushed into the west into the lands of the Cornish past the Tamar River. The biggest threat to his reign emerged in 937 when a loose confederation of Scots, Britons, Cumbrians, Irish, and Scandinavians came together to take on the ever-expanding military machine of Wessex.

As powerful as the Wessex army had become, the combined might of these desperate foes nearly undid all of Wessex's gains. This struggle culminated in the Battle of Brunanburh, which is remembered as one of the bloodiest in British history. Nevertheless, in the end, Æthelstan and his Wessex-based Anglo-Saxons were victorious and drove their enemies out. Æthelstan would perish two years later but would die knowing that his kingdom was secure.

Along with the decisive victory, it has been said the integral system of administration that Æthelstan put in place had much to do with the lasting success of Wessex and its successor state of

England. Æthelstan established a complex system of administrators who were all interconnected with each other and ready and willing to effectively carry out their duties.

From top to bottom, posts such as ealdorman, sheriff, and hundred-man ensured the kingdom was taken care of at every level. For instance, the hundred-man was in charge of a shire that consisted of roughly one hundred residents. Through this elaborate system, the lands of England were cut up into various sections and doled out. However, the people still remained connected to each other.

A rewards system was also put in place, in which those who loyally served the kingdom would be rewarded with land grants. This focus on gaining a landed estate would continue throughout English history. Further enshrinement of the universal legal code and systems of revenue accruement would also do much to keep the peace among citizens while ensuring the kingdom remained financially solvent. The system would hold firm, even under turbulent conditions, as was evidenced when Vikings temporarily seized York after Æthelstan's demise in 939.

However, this proved to be just a momentary relapse, as the stronger Wessex system pulled York back into its orbit by 954. As strong as the realm Alfred the Great had founded had become, it was faced with a grave new threat by the late 10th century. Renewed Viking raids—this time from Denmark—threatened to topple everything that Alfred the Great and his successors had built. This led to much of England coming under the rule of a Viking warlord known as Cnut the Great.

Norse armies, equipped with their huge broadswords and battleaxes, posed a ferocious threat to anyone who came across them. This struggle produced the Irish warrior Brian Boru, who fought several factions of Viking holdouts and became the high king of Ireland in 1002.

In England, a new star was rising in the form of Edward the Confessor. Edward, who was the son of Æthelred the Unready, had been invited to succeed the Norseman Harthacnut. He proved to be a powerful and unifying king.

Edward's reign was stable, but upon his death in 1066, new drama would ensue, this time from the shores of Normandy.

Edward did not have a direct heir, and William, Duke of Normandy, decided he was entitled to rule over the English throne. He said he was the grandson of King Edward's uncle, Richard II of Normandy. This claim was not recognized in England, and upon Edward's death, a nobleman named Harold Godwinson was named as the successor. Some say that Edward gave the throne to William or that Harold promised to support William's claim. There is no written proof of either of these claims, although William stated they happened.

William was willing to make his claim by force if necessary. The bold duke gathered a large army and crossed the Channel to invade England. Harold was crowned king of England on January 6th, 1066, and William of Normandy launched his invasion that September.

Just prior to William waging war, he tried his hand at diplomacy. Upon hearing of Harold being crowned, he wrote Harold directly, bringing before him his claim to the throne. However, Harold replied that it was not his decision to become the new king, reminding William that he had been chosen by the nobility. Harold basically tried to wash his hands of the dispute by claiming he was chosen and now must live out his obligations. But William, of course, would not accept this. After months of preparation, William and his forces landed on September 28th, 1066, at Pevensey, England.

He constructed a fortress right where he landed. William would oversee further operations from this beachhead. His efforts would culminate in the Battle of Hastings, which took place on October 14th, 1066. This titanic battle between the forces of William of Normandy and King Harold II decided who would rule England.

The two armies confronted each other some seven miles from the southeastern English town of Hastings. The two armies were both large, but King Harold's army was primarily infantry, whereas William had a professional cavalry and a strong contingent of archers. Harold was low on skilled soldiers because his armies had already been bled dry during two previous threats that he had to face shortly after he was crowned.

Harold had to fend off both a Viking incursion and a threat from his own brother, coming out on top in the Battle of Stamford Bridge. Stamford Bridge was about two hundred miles north of Hastings, and Harold and his forces made the journey in four days, an astounding feat.

To offset the deficit between William's skilled warriors and Harold's less experienced infantry, Harold attempted to launch a surprise attack against William to catch his army off-guard. However, his attempt was discovered, and Harold found William's army ready for him. The fighting began on the morning of October 14th and lasted until night fell.

A depiction of the Battle of Hastings as seen on the Bayeux Tapestry, a 230-foot-long and 20-foot-tall embroidered cloth that details the Norman conquest.
https://commons.wikimedia.org/wiki/File:Odo_bayeux_tapestry.png

The battle began with a mighty salvo from William's bowmen, who sent volley after volley of arrows into the English defensive lines. William's assault was followed by his men with lances, who charged ahead to mow down English positions. This charge was mostly ineffective and prompted William to send in the cavalry.

William's number one tactic during this exchange was to have his forces pretend as if they were getting ready to retreat at critical moments during the conflict. They would pull back, tricking their enemy into pursuing them, only to turn around and drop the hammer on top of them. This tactic was apparently used several times during the conflict. The battle finally came to an end when Harold fell in battle. His absence on the battlefield led his army to be routed.

The body was identified by his own mistress—Edith Swanneck or Edith the Fair—who just happened to be present on that day of carnage. It is said that she identified Harold's butchered corpse by way of marks on the body known only to her.

In the meantime, William had to prove to his own men that he was still alive. A rumor had spread through the ranks that William had fallen, leaving the men unsteady and ready to retreat. William rode around with his helmet turned up, showing his face and pointing at himself while shouting that he was still alive.

Back in England's halls of power, the fight continued. Shortly after word was received of Harold's demise, a new king was crowned: Edward the Confessor's great-nephew, Edgar Ætheling.

Edgar was young and inexperienced. He was a mere plaything of the noble class. William faced only minor resistance as he made his way farther inland. Ultimately, the token resistance of the nobility and their puppet king Edgar, who was never officially crowned, would surrender. William would end up being crowned as England's new king on December 25th, 1066.

However, the coronation did not exactly go as planned, as a disturbance was sparked over a common misunderstanding. William's Norman troops apparently heard the gathering crowd at Westminster Abbey shouting, "God save the King!" and misinterpreted it as a threat rather than a call to William's longevity. Fearing that an attack was imminent, they began torching surrounding structures in an attempt to drive off the mob. Despite this mishap, William was handed the English crown as planned.

There were still some loose ends to tie up, and further conquest of the rest of England would continue over the next few years. The veritable military occupation of Norman forces would last for about twenty years until all resistance was crushed. Perhaps it is no surprise that the more untamed lands to the north proved the hardest to subdue. The Normans took over much of Wales but never invaded Scotland, although Norman influence made its way north regardless.

Although Anglo-Saxon culture was overshadowed by the Norman culture, it would still continue. The Normans would rule England for three hundred years.

Chapter 2: Medieval Madness

*"There'll always be an England, while there's a country lane.
Wherever there's a cottage small beside a field of grain. There'll
always be an England. England shall be free ... If England means
as much to you as England means to me."*

-Vera Lynn

Although the Anglo-Saxons had been conquered by William,
Duke of Normandy, the social infrastructure they had established
was largely left in place. The Normans would largely replace the
Anglo-Saxons as landlords, but they abided by the same familiar
feudal system the Anglo-Saxons themselves had established,
although some have argued the Anglo-Saxon brand of feudalism
was more akin to outright slavery. The Normans, from whom we
get the official term "feudal" (*feu* is French for land), for the most
part, essentially just rebranded the practice.

Although it was most certainly a rude awakening for the Anglo-
Saxon elite to lose ownership of their lands, for the poorer classes
who labored on their estates, nothing much had changed except
for the fact they were suddenly under new management. That is
not to say there was not a general feeling of being occupied by a
foreign power among the lower classes.

The fact that their taskmasters were native French speakers had
the effect of making the native-born English feel at odds in their
own country. The language of power was now a foreign tongue

rather than the language of their birth. This sentiment was captured by a chronicler of that period, a monk named Orderic Vitalis. When writing about the Norman conquest, Orderic bluntly expressed, "Foreigners grew wealthy with the spoils of England while her own sons were either shamefully slain or driven as exiles to wander hopelessly through foreign kingdoms."

At any rate, in the Norman system of feudalism, the king was on top, and his nobles were below him. The most powerful nobles owned large tracts of land—they were the original "landlords." They, in turn, divvied up parts of their lands to lesser nobles. These lesser nobles granted lands to members of more respectable classes, such as knights and merchants, and in some instances, they rented portions of the land out.

The lowest class of society was landless and toiled on the estates of the rich landowners. They were almost entirely beholden to the will of their landlords. Like the Russian serfs, they were not free to leave the lands they worked and were destined to a life of backbreaking work for the nobility, who gave their workers meager shelter from the elements and a vague promise of protection should any outsider come and threaten them.

Under this system, the king was meant to be connected to all of his subjects in a solid chain from top to bottom. The king was also technically the default owner of all the lands in his realm. Although nobles could claim large estates and pass that land to their heirs, if a landowner found themselves in a situation in which land could not be passed on after their demise (for instance, if there was no heir apparent), that land would automatically become the king's possession. Daughters could receive land, but they sometimes needed a male retainer.

The system was much the same as what happens to modern-day properties with no one to claim them; if there is no claimant, those properties will eventually default to government ownership. In medieval England, it could be said that the king was the embodiment of the government, and if no one could actively claim a parcel of land, it would automatically revert to his direct control.

William the Conqueror proved to be a shrewd steward of properties and took this role very seriously. In 1086, he sent out a team of specialists to conduct a complex survey of the country to document who owned what and to estimate the value of their properties. This enabled William to effectively enact taxation that fairly represented the true status of the landholders in his domain. It even tallied up how many sheep and plows each landed estate had!

As intricate and effective as this survey was, it was deeply resented by the landed nobles, who felt they were being intruded upon and marched off to an unavoidable economic judgment. They even referred to the meticulously compiled survey as the Domesday Book in reference to the biblical Book of Revelation.

Despite the protests of the nobles, the end of the world was not near. But the end of William the Conqueror's reign was very well drawing nigh. The following year, in 1087, Norman King William perished. After William's passing, his son, William Rufus, was given control of England, while Normandy fell into the hands of William's other son, Robert.

The Crusades were kicking into high gear around this time. Shortly into Robert's reign over Normandy, he left to take part in the holy war brewing in the Middle East. He made sure to give William II charge over his dominion in his absence. On the surface, it probably seemed the greatest threat to stability would have been if Robert had perished while crusading. However, there was a greater threat. The younger William could have easily made Normandy a permanent vassal state, just as both England and Normandy had been under the control of his namesake and father, the late William the Conqueror.

But neither of these things happened. Robert survived the Crusades just fine. It was actually his brother, William, King of England, who perished first in 1100; Robert was returning from his crusade when he died. William did not die in some heated battle in a faraway land but rather in a freak hunting accident on his own estate. He was accidentally felled by an arrow. One of his brothers, Henry, was present at the time. Henry decided to seize the initiative rather than allow his crusading brother Robert to return and attempt to exert control. He rushed off to Winchester, took hold of the treasury, and was subsequently handed the crown just a few days thereafter.

Upon his return to Normandy, Robert, a veteran of the Crusades, was infuriated to hear of these underhanded happenings. He gathered his forces in Normandy and threatened to invade, just as his father had done all those years before. But since most of the nobles sided with Henry, there would be no repeat of the Battle of Hastings. Robert ultimately had to admit defeat. He agreed to remain in Normandy, and the threat of war seemed to be over.

However, Henry was convinced he could do more than bully his brother into submission. He decided to gather the bulk of his forces and invade Normandy itself. His invasion was a smashing success, and Robert was not only soundly defeated but also taken prisoner. As a result, Normandy and England were once again reunited—this time under the sole rule of King Henry. This was Henry's greatest triumph, and for the rest of his reign, he became obsessed with the idea of being able to pass his vast territorial holdings to one heir.

These aims were squashed when Henry's son and heir apparent perished in a mishap on the high seas in 1120. Henry would reign for several more years and ultimately designate his daughter, Matilda, as his heir. Matilda was married to a powerful French noble named Geoffrey Plantagenet, who controlled a sizeable section of France called Anjou. Henry was always keen on expanding his kingdom and hoped this connection would help merge Anjou with the territory his daughter Matilda was set to inherit.

But as is often the case with the best-laid plans of mice and monarchs, things did not turn out as King Henry had wished. After his passing, his daughter Matilda ended up fighting for control against another claimant, Henry's nephew, Stephen of Blois. In the ensuing crisis, Matilda lost popular support, and the nobility ended up siding with Stephen. Even so, Matilda tried to hang on, leading to an all-out civil war that rocked England for over a decade.

The Anarchy, where England suffered a breakdown in law and order, was resolved in 1153 when Stephen and Matilda called for a truce and hammered out an agreement in which Stephen would be recognized as monarch on the condition that Matilda's son,

Henry, would be allowed to wear the crown after Stephen's death. Surprisingly enough, the promise to give Matilda's son the crown was honored. Upon Stephen's demise, Henry II became the first king of England to enjoy an entirely peaceful transition of power in quite some time.

An image of Henry II.
https://commons.wikimedia.org/wiki/File:Henry_II_Plantagenet.jpg

Henry was also blessed to come to prominence at a time of great progress in medieval England. Great strides had been made in many fields of industry. Around this time, horseshoes and collars were being developed to ease the burden and increase the productivity of horses. These developments, in turn, led to the development of horse-drawn plows, which proved to be far more proficient than the older variation of oxen-driven plows.

These advancements greatly increased the output of crops, giving England a great boost to its agricultural stability. Under Henry's reign, watermills were developed, allowing the grinding of grain by way of hydropower. Roads were also much more reliable at this time, and greater travel was achieved, enabling stronger networks of commerce between the various parts of Henry's kingdom.

Along with these general improvements, King Henry II also made improvements in the rule of law by shifting legal jurisdiction from regional "baronial courts," which were not known for fairness or impartiality, to his own royal courts. The king's courts used a jury system of twelve jurors to determine the outcome of cases, enabling a much fairer verdict than the lopsided ones that barons had been arbitrarily handing out.

Those in a real bind knew they could appeal their case to the king's court to get a fair hearing. The system certainly was not perfect, but as the current writer and historian Simon Schama put it, "Nonetheless, it was still an immeasurable advance on the feudal monopoly of justice common elsewhere in baronial Europe." Perhaps the most important development occurred toward the beginning of the 12th century when judges of all regions began to rely upon a uniform standard of law.

Such things, no doubt, seem like a given to most of us in the modern world today, but prior to this development, it was anything but. Before the development of what was ultimately termed "common law," one could find the rules and regulations varying wildly; it depended on who was interpreting the law. A lasting tradition of uniformity was established through common law, and this same sense of needing a universal legal code was ultimately gifted to Britain's later colonies, including those that would one day become the United States of America.

The city of London saw enormous growth during the 12th century. By the 1150s, London was becoming a bustling center for both commerce and political wrangling. The city was often divided into sections based on class, and depending on where you were, you could run into either corner markets hawking basic meats to the peasants or find delicatessens selling finer upscale items such as venison to the richer citizens who could afford it.

Henry II would be succeeded by the famous Richard the Lionheart, who spent more time away crusading in the Holy Land than actually ruling England. The heirless Richard was succeeded by his brother, John. Today, King John is often viewed as a corrupt monarch who took advantage of the feudal system. In those days, the nobility had their own local courts where they exacted fines against those who had transgressed local ordinances.

John was known to purposefully bounce local court cases up to the king's court, which he was personally in charge of, in an effort to bilk as many resources from the court proceedings as possible. John also increased the fees paid by inheritors of land to line his own pockets.

Under the feudal system, it was customary for one about to inherit the land that had been lorded over by their forebearers to pay a small fee to the king to make the inheritance official. John was known to greedily jack up these fees to bolster his own finances. This was viewed as both greedy and miserly in the extreme. King John was already rich, and yet here he was, repeatedly trying to suck his subjects dry. He also taxed local merchants at unheard-of exorbitant rates. It is safe to say that King John was not very popular with the masses.

The only saving grace of such a harsh taskmaster was the fact that the king and his armies had pledged to protect the lives and properties of his subjects from any outside threat. But John proved he could not fulfill this basic duty in 1204, as the king of France managed to seize hold of Normandy, thereby forcing countless members of the nobility to forfeit their estates.

In the end, these embittered nobles realized King John had milked them for what they were worth by taking full advantage of the feudal system but could not even hold up his part of the bargain by protecting them from outside invasions. If there was such a thing as poll numbers for British monarchs back in medieval times, King John's approval rate would have been terrible.

The pope took notice. Sensing how weak King John was, he decided to engage in some power playing of his own. John had previously resisted the pope's pick for the archbishop of Canterbury, but the pope was now ready to throw down the gauntlet in order for his demands to be met. He excommunicated King John, essentially giving his blessing to the king of France to launch an invasion of England.

The pope then took the extraordinary measure of ordering every church in England to shut its doors. A complete shutdown of churches in those days was a very serious matter. If folks could not go to church, they felt their very soul was in mortal danger. Due to the outside aggression from France and the internal pressures of shuttered churches, King John finally submitted to the pope's demands and allowed his pick for the archbishop of Canterbury to go forward in 1213.

King John had apparently made a mockery of feudalism, and from the nobility to the peasantry, his subjects were fed up. While King John was backed into a corner, a sizeable portion of the nobility presented him with an ultimatum for reform, which would ultimately become known as the Magna Carta. Often recognized as a forerunner for other major documents of political reform, such as the Constitution of the United States, the Magna Carta was drafted to ensure certain rights and freedoms would be respected by the king.

The Magna Carta from 1215. It is one of only four left in existence. You can see this document in the British Library.
https://en.wikipedia.org/wiki/File:Magna_Carta_(British_Library_Cotton_MS_Augustus_II.106).jpg

The document ensured, among other things, that English subjects (at least landed subjects) would have a fair and legal trial if prosecuted. Subjects were also protected against unwarranted abuse by the king's subordinates. Although this document would later be used as a model for even greater freedoms, it was not very effective at the time, as war still broke out. But it had been cobbled together by a frustrated nobility as a means to keep their troublesome king within the well-recognized limits of feudal society.

In that sense, it was created more to ensure the status quo than to achieve radical reforms, but it still paved the way for greater freedoms to come. Although it was a long evolutionary process, the establishment of the Magna Carta can be said to be the beginning of the end of feudalism in England.

Feudal life had previously been ruled by a sovereign monarch who was the underlying owner of all the land. Other people could be landlords but only with the approval of the king, which meant their land could essentially be taken from them at any time. With the Magna Carta, there were clear rules and regulations in place to limit the scope of the monarch's power. The eventual balance between Parliament and the monarchy would be achieved through fine-tuning the details of this revolutionary document.

From this point forward, England would have a series of kings who either granted concessions based on the Magna Carta or attempted to dial back the reforms of this pivotal document to better foster absolutist rule. But no matter what happened or who was in charge, for the rest of English history, the nobility of the land continuously sought to hold their leaders accountable.

Another great change in feudal society at this time was the noble class's refusal to wage the king's wars for free. In the past, the king reserved the absolute right to call the nobility to fight in his wars for a period of no less than forty days. The nobility demanded an end to this practice, and the English kings from here on out were forced to pay their troops, which led to many ramifications in the future.

Most notably, the eventual successor to the English Crown—Henry III—would have a horrible time finding enough money to fund his wars. He resorted to taxation, but his stringent measures led the nobility to revolt against him. During Henry III's reign, the First English Parliament convened in 1258 when the frustrated nobility, led by a powerful earl named Simon de Montfort,

brought the leading lights of England togethe
conspire against the king.

The coronation of Henry III.
https://commons.wikimedia.org/wiki/File:HenryIII.jpg

Simon, who spoke French, referred to the meeting with the Old French word *parlement*, which means "speaking" or "discussion." Just think of the phrase, "Parlez-vous français?" and you will get the idea of why Simon de Montfort called it a *parlement*. The establishment of Parliament led to the English monarch losing even more power, as the noble class took control of the treasury, got their hands on the tools of taxation, and began to dictate to the monarch about who should be his advisors.

Henry III and his son, Edward I, were able to defeat Simon de Montfort on the battlefield in 1265, but ironically enough, the English Parliament he had helped establish would not be defeated so easily. And the newfound rights and privileges of the nobility would remain intact. Henry's successor, Edward I, respected Parliament. He knew the nobility's power and typically tried to appease Parliament rather than antagonize it.

A portrait thought to be of Edward I.
https://commons.wikimedia.org/wiki/File:Edward_I_-_Westminster_Abbey_Sedilia.jpg

Edward worked with the nobility to establish a representative legislative body. In 1275, King Edward I ordered every region to assign two designated representatives to stand for them in Parliament. This was the beginning of "representation" in light of regional "taxation." American revolutionaries at the Boston Tea Party would cry out a similar phrase. By the time of Edward's rule, people realized that if they were being taxed by the Crown, they deserved some form of representation in Parliament.

Another blow to feudalism was the decline in vassals. The poor classes were beginning to no longer be chained to the land they worked on. They were gaining more freedom of mobility. Landlords increasingly recruited the leaders of the peasantry to serve as their eyes and ears on their property. Peasants were hired to collect rents and oversee properties, establishing traditional roles like jurors, reeves, and haywards. Some of these positions exist in altered forms today. The modern-day equivalent of a reeve, for example, would be a chief magistrate.

Placing local peasants in property management positions had several benefits. First of all, no one knew the peasantry better than a peasant. Therefore, recruiting from the peasant class ensured that a manager was equipped with adequate knowledge of the life and culture of those who rented out land and toiled on the estate.

Peasant managers also "softened" the image of the feudal system. Toiling away on the land of the elites did not seem as harsh if the main taskmaster the peasants interacted with was one of their own or someone from a similar background. It also promoted the idea that they could move up the social ladder.

But one of the most fundamental changes to medieval society was not reforms. It was not initiated by the peasantry or the landed elite. Rather, it was a horrible plague known as the Black Death.

This scourge struck England in the middle of the 14th century under the leadership of King Edward III. King Edward III would be affected by the plague early on, as his daughter Joan perished from the dreaded illness. Joan had been traveling through Bordeaux, France, to meet and marry her fiancé, Peter (Pedro) of Castile, in Spain. However, there would be no marriage. Her grieving father would write to his attendants, "No fellow human being could be surprised if we were inwardly desolated by the sting of this bitter grief for we are human too."

The plague that had afflicted Joan had been spreading throughout southern Europe for some time, and it reached England via its southern ports. Although Edward was certainly not a scientist who understood the spread of a pathogen, he at least recognized where the disease entered the country, as he immediately sent the archbishop of Canterbury to offer penitential prayers at Kent since the southern ports had become home to the plague.

The ports of the world were indeed passing along more than merchandise. The plague is believed to have originated somewhere in the Near East and was then imported to the Mediterranean by visiting merchant craft. It spread like wildfire throughout southern Europe until it was finally picked up by additional travelers and sent farther abroad to Britain, impacting Wales, England, and Scotland. The illness spread rapidly, and whole villages were soon decimated by the Black Death.

Many felt what they were experiencing was nothing short of the end of the world. And since just about everything in those days was viewed through the lens of religion, many could not help but think that God was somehow punishing them. Ironically enough, just prior to the plague, the world was taking part in an overall boon in prosperity and a population explosion. So many people crowded together in close quarters would aid in the plague's transmission, which would ultimately reduce the biggest population centers of Europe.

Rats have long been blamed for spreading the plague, but due to the rapid spread of the disease, it seems far more likely that humans were the hosts of infected fleas and lice. All it took was one bite from an infected flea to become infected.

People were also not as aware of the benefits of hygiene as we are today, which allowed the disease to spread more easily. The disease went largely unnoticed until the symptoms became more pronounced. The symptoms were terrible. Those afflicted with the Black Death broke out in boils from head to toe. Painful buboes, or swollen lymph nodes, were filled with puss. People also developed a hacking cough and terrible fever. Soon into this infection, the victim would find themselves losing almost all of their energy until they were finally consigned to just staying in bed. And soon after that, most would lose their entire will to live.

Those who could live out their last days in a sick bed cared for by a loved one were, of course, the lucky ones. English chronicler Thomas Burton would later write, "The pestilence grew so strong that men and women dropped dead in the streets." There was, in essence, a complete breakdown of society. As simplistic as medieval life might have been compared to our modern-day world, the effect the illness had on everyday life was devastating all the same.

For example, those in the cities were accustomed to buying bread from local bakeries. But with bakers and their employees dying by the dozen, they found their local baker's shelves bare.

Even the grisly fact that there were so many dead bodies lying around was a reminder of this breakdown. Normally, there would have been someone on hand to immediately remove the bodies of those who had perished, yet with so many sick and dying—and others unwilling to go near diseased corpses—there was suddenly no one to pick up the dead.

English chronicler William Dene wrote about this misery, saying, "Alas, this mortality devoured such a multitude of both sexes that no one could be found to carry the bodies of the dead to burial, but men and women carried the bodies of their own little ones to church on their shoulders and threw them into mass graves from which arose such a stench that it was barely possible for anyone to go past the churchyard." Perhaps it is an incredible understatement, but it must have been a truly terrible sight to behold.

The large number of deceased also put a considerable strain on the church since it was hard for priests to keep up with the growing death toll. Prior to the plague, a priest giving someone their last rites was considered very important. But the realities of such massive casualties made it impossible to carry this tradition on like normal.

Instead, the church began to make great concessions, encouraging those who could not have access to a priest to confess their sins to a lay person. Before, only a priest could hear one's confession, but due to the dire circumstances, with priests sick, dying, or unwilling to visit plague houses, it was deemed suitable for the average person to serve as a replacement.

This demonstrated that religious rules were not always set in stone. It could be said that this initial chipping away at the rigid religious structure may have laid down some of the groundwork for England's later reformation. At any rate, after the first onslaught of the plague had subsided, many were left questioning just about every aspect of medieval life.

There were deep thinkers who questioned religion and the nature of reality. Other, perhaps more practical thinkers questioned the unsanitary conditions of English cities. The latter was of the belief (and there was some truth in their estimations) that the cramped, dirty cities were becoming breeding grounds for illness and disease.

In their critique, they cited the filthy streets that often had both animal and human waste flowing down them every time it rained. And they cited the foggy, baleful air of London, fearing that some terrible "miasma" of illness was hanging over their heads. Although these critiques of city life were not completely scientific in their analysis, they were on the right track. If cities like London were not so unsanitary, the citizens might have fared a little better during this terrible episode.

King Edward III, to his credit, recognized as much and enacted street cleaning measures to be carried out in London. Much of it was too little, too late.

In the aftermath of the Black Death, there was a distinct shift in the public's thinking. The old social order of medieval times had been irrevocably shattered. For the peasants in the countryside who were not directly affected by the plague, they found themselves virtually abandoned by the nobles and lords who had sworn to protect them.

Those with money had fled to more remote, isolated estates in a bid to stay alive. With their taskmasters gone, the old social contract of peasants toiling on lands in exchange for the protection of the nobility had been broken. The peasants were left on their own. If they wished to protect what little they had from roving thieves, they would have to do it themselves. This created a greater degree of self-sufficiency and a streak of independence that would only continue to grow.

Chapter 3: Enter the Tudors

"In England there are sixty different religions, and only one sauce."

-Francesco Caracciolo

King Edward III inherited a large, sprawling kingdom. And throughout all of the trials and tribulations England had faced, he was determined to increase his prestige further.

Edward was a lover of knights and chivalry. During a court appearance in 1348, a lady of the court accidentally lost her garter. Edward let his chivalrous nature take over. While others laughed, he simply picked it up and wrapped it around his own leg, stating, "Let him be ashamed who sees wrong in it."

This legendary act of rescuing a mortified damsel from utter embarrassment led to the establishment of the Order of the Garter. The order consisted of twenty-four knights and acted in a similar fashion as King Arthur's Round Table.

King Edward III passed away in 1377. After the passing of this chivalrous and larger-than-life ruler, the English crown was handed to Edward's grandson, Richard II.

Edward's funerary monument.
https://commons.wikimedia.org/wiki/File:Edward-III-king-England.jpg

Richard's reign would soon run into trouble when an attempt to raise taxes led to an open rebellion among the peasant classes. The protest was led by Wat Tyler, and the poor people stood up as one and declared they were all "formed in Christ's likeness" and should be treated equally. One can easily hear echoes of this proclamation for equality hundreds of years later in America's Declaration of Independence.

The Declaration of Independence similarly proclaims, "We hold these truths to be self-evident, that all men are created equal, that they are endowed by their Creator with certain unalienable rights, that among these are Life, Liberty, and the Pursuit of Happiness." It also proclaims that "all men are created equal under God."

The Peasant's Revolt under Tyler was as rapid as it was shocking. It ran its course in just a few weeks, but during that time, the peasant masses managed to seize much of London. It was only after the ringleader, Wat Tyler, was killed that the situation changed. But his death wasn't the end of the protests; rather, it served as a signal to King Richard II that it was time for a compromise.

After Tyler was killed, the situation became untenable, with folks rioting in the streets. King Richard II no longer had the stomach for any more discontent. He let it be known that he would agree to many of the protesters' demands if they went home and allowed the reforms to take shape. It was a strong order, but many in the mob realized this was likely their best opportunity. A king's word was golden, and they had King Richard II making them promises.

As such, they decided to give it a chance and see what compromises could be made. Many reforms were passed, and many of the demands of the peasants were met. But even so, things did not go so well for King Richard, as he was forcefully removed from power in 1399.

After his removal, another succession crisis took place since Richard II had no immediate heir. The only real contender was Edward III's great-grandson, Edmund Mortimer, Earl of March. The other contender was Richard's cousin, Henry of Lancaster, who was the child of a nobleman who traced his lineage back to King Edward III's paternal grandmother.

Henry (also known as Henry Bolingbroke) was the one responsible for Richard's removal. Henry had been previously exiled by Richard II for plotting against the king during an uprising in 1388. In 1399, Henry rallied a substantial number of supporters. He returned to England and forced King Richard II off the throne.

Henry IV was officially crowned king in Westminster Abbey on October 13th, 1399. Upon gaining the crown, he would be dubbed Henry IV. Despite frequent domestic turmoil, King Henry IV made impressive waves on the international level. In December 1400, he even gained the distinction of being the only English king to play host to a visiting Byzantine emperor, Manuel II Palaiologos.

Henry IV perished in 1413, and his son, Henry V, took over. After a brief reign, Henry V passed away in 1422 and was succeeded by his infant son, Henry VI. This infant king would face more strife than his predecessors. For most of his reign, King Henry VI was knee-deep in the Hundred Years' War between England and France.

Any recollection of English history would be remiss without at least a brief mention of the Hundred Years' War and its role in shaping England. This war was one of the greatest conflagrations to affect Europe during the Late Middle Ages. It was a series of constant conflicts that spanned from 1337 to 1453.

Although the war had some rather complicated threads, all strands led back to a long-standing dispute between English and French claimants to the French throne. The two claimants—the English House of Plantagenet and the French House of Valois— went to war to assert their claims to the French throne and other territorial disputes. The war would carry on from one king to another, with both sides continuing to insist their claims be recognized. The fighting only ceased when the House of Valois emerged victorious, retaining its hold on France.

The seemingly endless fighting on behalf of royal claimants might seem rather absurd and pointless to us from a modern perspective. But nevertheless, the conflict had lasting effects on Europe. For one thing, the constant fighting ensured the armies of western Europe developed into highly efficient standing armies, and impressive new innovations, such as artillery, were perfected.

But back to our subject at hand: King Henry VI. Henry VI was not necessarily a bad king, but he was not very effective as a ruler, especially when it came to rapidly unfolding situations like internal unrest and external warfare. His inner circle felt he was not up for the job and began to plot against him. In light of Henry VI's abject weakness, several noble families became increasingly powerful; since they often provided troops, they also had their own standing armies. The leading lights of the nobility sought to take King Henry VI down. The conflict that ensued is known as the Wars of the Roses.

In 1461, Edward IV, the son of the duke of York, defeated the royal forces and locked Henry VI in the Tower of London. After nine years on the throne, an army led by the Lancastrian family defeated Edward, forcing him to flee and put Henry back on the throne. However, this change on the throne did not last long, as

Edward would again raise troops and knock Henry VI off the throne in 1471. Henry VI was placed in the Tower of London and perished shortly thereafter.

The drama continued when Edward IV died in 1483. His brother, Richard of Gloucester, was the lord protector of Edward V, Edward IV's son and heir. However, the young Edward V and his brother mysteriously disappeared, with many believing Richard had ordered their deaths. Richard took the throne in 1483, only to be challenged just a couple of years later in 1485. This challenge was lodged by Henry Tudor.

Henry was willing to take the crown by force if necessary. He cobbled together an army and took the fight directly to Richard. Even though Tudor's army of five thousand was dwarfed by Richard's army of eight thousand, Henry's troops fought ferociously. Henry Tudor defeated Richard in battle and was crowned King Henry VII, ushering in the first king of the Tudor dynasty.

A portrait of King Henry VII.
https://commons.wikimedia.org/wiki/File:Henry_Seven_England.jpg

In many ways, King Henry VII was a man of the people and tried to craft policies that were beneficial for the growing body of farmers and merchants. Unlike his predecessors, who focused on war and expansion, Henry VII looked inward at his realm and sought to improve England's commercial might. This led to England finally having a monarch who sought to avoid conflicts. Henry VII used all of his skills in diplomacy to avoid conflict with both Scotland and France. Rather than fighting violent wars, King Henry VII found himself in a trade war with the Hanseatic League.

The Hanseatic League was a conglomeration of merchant guilds based out of northern Europe; it was particularly situated in German-speaking lands. The Hanseatic League had a decisive impact on English trade, as it essentially closed England off from trading partners in the regions where the Hanseatic League held a monopoly. England was also facing a decline in trade with France and Italy. However, King Henry VII was able to cement a trade deal with the Netherlands that opened up the door for greater and more robust trade with the rest of Europe.

Another way King Henry VII helped to ensure stability was by stipulating that only he could have his own army. Such a thing seems like common sense today (why would you let the powerful people of society have their own soldiers?), but prior to King Henry VII's ascension to the throne, just about every noble family on the block had their own standing army.

Rather than shoring up the nobility's support, Henry VII did his best to gain the backing of the merchant and guild classes, which were essentially the middle classes of England at the time. They, like him, sought prosperity over conflict and appreciated the king's efforts to avoid war while bolstering the economic output of England.

The only thing that King Henry VII was willing to spend an excessive amount of money on was the outfitting of a new fleet of merchant craft. He did this with the foresight of knowing that England's success would depend on being able to travel across the high seas to trade with other nations. Due to Henry VII's wise stewardship, by the time of his passing in 1509, England was financially solvent and poised for even greater economic success.

His successor, Henry VIII, had a very solid foundation upon which to build.

A portrait of King Henry VIII.

Henry VIII was not as financially minded as his father. He had no problem at all with spending money. Not long into his reign, Henry VIII commissioned the expensive remodeling of Richmond Palace, making it one of the most luxurious in Europe. However, to his credit, King Henry VIII was, in many ways, a great showman who understood the importance of maintaining a popular public image. And part of his ostentatious showiness was an effort to gain public affection.

Aiding him in gaining the public's interest was the fact this young king decided to marry early on, wedding a beautiful and socially prominent woman by the name of Catherine of Aragon. Just as royal weddings today galvanize the public in Britain and beyond, the same could be said back in the days of King Henry VIII. And his marriage to Catherine of Aragon was certainly a public relations boon.

Although Henry VIII's father was an able steward, he was a quiet man who did not do much to excite the general public.

Seeing the crowning of a young king and his marriage to the Spanish princess was very exciting for the public. The new king and queen presented themselves to their subjects in an elaborate coronation ceremony on June 23rd, 1509. All of this pomp and ceremony was like a breath of fresh air for an England that had grown somewhat weary of its previous king. Although Henry VII had been financially solvent, he was reclusive.

As refreshing as the coronation of Henry VIII might have been, there were some loose ends to tie up from the previous administration. His father had implemented a special task force named the Council Learned in the Law, which was in charge of securing payment of debt. If the title "Council Learned in the Law" does not sound arrogant and presumptuous enough ("learned in the law: is just another way to say "know it all"), the most effective councilors on this task force had rubbed the public the wrong way.

In particular, two of the most brutal enforcers—Richard Empson and Edmund Dudley—had provoked the people's ire. These two were extreme in their measures of extracting what they wanted from their targets and, at times, even overstepped the bounds of the fairly broad legal authority they had been given. The council carried over into King Henry VIII's reign, but it was incredibly unpopular.

Both Empson and Dudley had already faced prosecution for allegedly overstepping their authority by the time of King Henry VIII's coronation. So, it was up to him to decide what to do with his father's most overzealous ministers. Should he pardon them or let them hang? Ultimately, the two were executed on charges of treason. It is not known if Henry fully endorsed their demise, but he certainly did not stop it.

Some historians have made the cynical observation that King Henry VIII might have learned a "valuable lesson" from this ordeal, as he learned how easy it was to assuage public discontent by punishing one small element of the kingdom's governance. If the public was upset with the direction things were going, instead of blaming the king, their blame could be directed at a small group of ministers instead.

Besides these two scapegoats, Henry kept most of his father's ministers, and they were able to competently steer the royal ship, regardless of Henry VIII's own aptitude for leadership. His most trusted advisor would soon emerge in the form of one Thomas Wolsey. Wolsey began his career as a priest and served as a chaplain in Canterbury before ministering directly to the royal court.

Upon taking the throne, Henry VIII recognized Wolsey's talent and made him the almoner, which meant Wolsey was in charge of all the alms being collected for the neediest members of the realm. After taking note of his effectiveness, Henry VIII decided to promote Wolsey directly into his inner circle in 1511. Thomas Wolsey proved himself a very efficient minister, and in 1515, he was made lord chancellor. Henry was so fond of Wolsey that he even pulled some strings to have the pope arrange for Wolsey to become his personal legate in England.

With powerful ministers like Thomas Wolsey in place, King Henry VIII largely let his governmental machinery run itself while he pursued his own interests in life. His greatest interest was to produce a male heir to the throne. He and his wife Catherine tried for several years, but the pair seemed unable to do so. Catherine did give birth to a healthy daughter named Mary, but all of the other children she birthed failed to survive.

Still seeking a son, Henry's roving, impatient eyes began to look elsewhere. Henry had already been unfaithful to his wife, having indulged in a wide variety of mistresses, but even he had to follow some semblance of protocol. And no matter how many sons he might produce out of wedlock, none of them would ever be accepted as a legitimate heir. This meant that if Henry wanted a legitimate son, he had to be born within the bounds of marriage. Henry realized he would have to somehow put away his wife Catherine and marry someone new in the hopes that his new bride could (hopefully) give birth to a son.

Henry's troubling desire to have a legitimate male heir would have him bending age-old rules and traditions. Interestingly enough, Henry rationalized his decision to put Catherine to the side by pointing to the Bible. He picked out some verses from the Book of Leviticus, which read, in part, "If a man shall take his brother's wife, it is an impunity: he hath uncovered his brother's nakedness: they shall be childless."

This verse resonated with Henry VIII since Catherine had been wed to Henry's unfortunate older brother, who perished in his teens shortly after his (apparently unconsummated) marriage. Henry reasoned that he had wrongly taken his brother's wife, violating a biblical prohibition, and was therefore being punished by being made to "be childless." It was a rather ingenious bit of religious-based rationalization on Henry's part, and it is possible that he actually believed it to be a valid reason.

With this convenient rationale in hand, Henry began entreating Pope Clement VII to issue an annulment to his marriage to Catherine of Aragon. Henry was not asking for a divorce; instead, he wished to make it as if his twenty-year marriage to Catherine did not exist and was never valid in the first place. If the annulment was granted, Henry was ready to put Catherine in a convent so that she would no longer have to live with the "shame" of having been in an improper relationship.

The execution of these arrangements fell on the shoulders of King Henry's favorite minister, Thomas Wolsey, who just so happened to be England's papal legate. Wolsey would not have been too sad to see Catherine go since he had long had an antagonistic relationship with the queen. She was an outspoken critic of some of Wolsey's policies and his excessive spending habits.

In addition to getting rid of Catherine's unwanted critiques, Wolsey saw an opportunity to arrange a marriage between King Henry and a French princess, thereby uniting England in a bond of friendship with a previously troublesome and unpredictable neighbor. Little did Wolsey know that Henry already had his heart set on a veteran of his court: Anne Boleyn.

Nevertheless, Wolsey dutifully did his part and began the process of petitioning the pope for an official annulment. There would be much unforeseen difficulty in achieving this feat. The pope was typically fairly compliant with England's wishes since Pope Clement viewed the English king as a loyal ally. Yet, the pope had his hands tied since he was also beholden to the Holy Roman emperor, Charles V, who was directly related to Catherine of Aragon (she was his aunt).

Stuck between a rock and a hard place, the pope had to figure out which monarch would do the worst damage if he offended them. Considering the size and power of the Holy Roman Empire, which comprised much of central Europe, in addition to Spain (Charles V was also king of Spain at the time), Pope Clement logically determined the repercussions of offending Charles V would have been much more severe. As such, he began the process of letting King Henry VIII know that there would be no annulment. He wanted to let the king down gently in a diplomatic and polite fashion.

Back in England, Catherine had figured out what her husband was up to and was beyond frustrated. One can, of course, understand her wrath. But in those days, women had few recourses against their husband's whims even under normal circumstances, let alone when their husband was the king of England. Thus, there was not a whole lot that she could do about it. She certainly could not punish her husband for his actions. But she could direct her scorn on someone else. Thomas Wolsey was the perfect target.

Since Wolsey was an instrument of the king, she took her wrath out on him. Although Wolsey was only following the king's orders, Catherine suspected that he had a personal motivation in carrying out these orders in light of her previous disapproval of him. In 1527, the pope, still unwilling to offer up a firm answer, decided to buy more time by advising papal legate Wolsey to convene a court in England to look into the matter further.

Wolsey was made the head of this court, thereby lending great hope that the annulment would go forward as planned. But little did anyone realize the long game that Pope Clement—a member of a famous family of political strategists, the Medicis—was playing.

However, King Henry was not placated by the show of cooperation that the pope displayed. Giving voice to his suspicions, he sent out threatening feelers to the Vatican, hinting that if things did not go as he intended, he might have to break from the Catholic Church entirely. Such suggestions were not taken lightly, considering the fact that Europe was in the full grip of the Protestant Reformation at the time. The greatest irony in all of this was that King Henry VIII was not at all in line with the Protestants.

King Henry had once been dubbed a "defender of the faith" by the pope. He was a staunch supporter of the Catholic doctrine. The sole reason for his proposed break with the Catholic Church was not due so much to a difference in religious beliefs but rather anger with the pope for not allowing him to have his way as it pertained to his marriage. Incredibly enough, it would be the self-interest of one king that ultimately led to England's first fissure with the Roman Catholic Church.

It was at this point that Wolsey began to become deeply troubled by the course that events seemed to be taking. His fears of a real rupture between England and the Catholic Church were expressed in a heartfelt letter to the pope in 1528. In contemplation of a real rift between Henry and the church, Wolsey agonized, "I close my eyes before such horror."

Several more lines of saddened reflection later, he ended this plea for cooperation, saying, "I throw myself at the Holy Father's feet." Wolsey was in a tough position, but he understood King Henry would be the hardest mountain to move as it pertained to keeping the peace. He knew that Henry VIII's mind was made up and that there was absolutely nothing he could do to make him reconsider.

So, Wolsey looked to the pope, believing him to be a more pliant individual with whom to reason. However, Pope Clement was in some rather dire straits. The previous year, Holy Roman Emperor Charles V's forces had marched on Rome, forcing the pope to seek refuge in his fortress of Castel Sant'Angelo.

Charles V was not directly responsible for this event. The situation was, in large part, one that had spiraled out of control. In the lead-up to this debacle, the armies of France and the Holy Roman Empire had been skirmishing in northern Italy for quite some time while the pope attempted to strategically place himself on the winning side. The papacy did come out on top when their ally, the Holy Roman Empire, defeated France. But in the immediate aftermath, HRE troops remained stationed in northern Italy. This prolonged occupation led to severe resentment among the locals on the ground. And the longer the troops were there, the more this resentment grew.

The imperial troops were also agitated by their prolonged stay and lack of appropriate provisions. Given enough time, this powder keg was bound to blow. Charles V did not even have to issue a command for war to erupt between his troops and local forces, culminating in the sack of Rome.

Although he did not authorize it, Holy Roman Emperor Charles V was savvy (or perhaps devious) enough to take advantage of the situation. Although aligned with the church, Charles V had already had his differences with the current pope, the biggest of which was a late-breaking development that the pope was in talks with France and apparently ready to switch sides! Now that this untrustworthy pontiff was literally backed into a corner, Charles V found himself in a position of unparalleled strength and leverage over the Vatican, and he was not going to let go too easily.

Needless to say, given the fact the pope was at the complete mercy of Holy Roman Emperor Charles V, he was not in a good position to anger him. He certainly could not sanction England's king to cast aside Charles V's aunt, Catherine of Aragon. Despite his inability to grant the annulment, the pope saw a strong potential ally in England, one that could save the papacy from the Holy Roman Empire. So, the pope continued to dither and delay, unwilling to make a final decision and ceaselessly playing these two sides against each other.

In the meantime, a court of inquiry convened in England, which was led by Wolsey, and attempted to find a possible alternative to Henry's annulment. Reconciliation between Henry and Catherine was mentioned, but it was, of course, immediately shot down. Henry did not need reconciliation—he needed a son. And he was certain no amount of marriage counseling could bring him that.

As the participants of the proceedings continued to try and find alternatives, it has been said that Catherine was asked to take a vow of chastity and join the convent as a nun to free Henry to remarry. However, strong-willed Catherine refused to do any such thing. She stated she would only join a convent if her husband joined a monastery and became a monk!

King Henry VIII took his case to the British public by making a series of passionate, emotional statements. In front of gatherings, he stated how much he loved his wife but that he had to follow the rules if it was ordained by the special court that his marriage to Catherine must be annulled. Henry was obviously attempting to win the people to his side so that when the announcement was made, he could appear as an innocent bystander meekly abiding by the divine ruling rather than one orchestrating the whole thing behind the scenes.

In 1529, another great twist in this ever-complicated story occurred, as a false report reached England saying that Pope Clement had died. If true, this would have meant a new pope would need to be selected. Almost immediately, King Henry VIII encouraged his trusted advisor and fixer, Thomas Wolsey, to throw his hat into the papal election. Wolsey was the papal legate in England, so he was already a powerful member of the clergy, but winning the seat of the papacy would have seemed like too great a leap for him. But if his king encouraged it, he was willing to make an attempt.

Ultimately, Wolsey did not have to do so because King Henry VIII would soon learn that Pope Clement did not die but was merely very sick. Clement recovered from his illness and continued to stand as an impediment to King Henry's desire for an annulment.

Around this time, Emperor Charles V defeated his nemesis, the French king, and restored the pope to Rome. With the pope under his thumb, Charles V became a direct benefactor. Clement would have found it impossible to cross him. So, in the end, the pope let Henry know he would not approve of the annulment after all.

Henry was infuriated. Almost immediately, he took his wrath out on the pope's closest representative—papal legate Thomas Wolsey. Wolsey was summoned to the king's court, where he knew he would likely be sentenced to execution. However, Wolsey apparently could not handle the stress. Incredibly enough, he perished of his own accord en route to the proceedings. If King Henry felt bad for what had happened to his old friend, it did not seem to show.

Instead, Henry charged full steam ahead with his plans. He began to push for a break with Rome and to have the king of England become the official head of the church. This directive was later made official in 1534 with the Act of Supremacy, which was approved by Parliament.

After putting Catherine away, Henry raced off to wed Anne Boleyn, whom he married in 1533. Things would not go so well for this new Tudor marriage. Even though Anne would bear Henry another daughter, the future Queen Elizabeth, her failure to give birth to a son resulted in her own execution in 1536.

Henry VIII was more than ready to move on and found a new wife, Jane Seymour, whom he wed less than two weeks later, on May 30th, 1536.

Jane would succeed where others had failed, giving birth to a male heir, Edward, on October 12th, 1537. However, Jane would not live to receive Henry's praise. She perished about two weeks after due to complications that occurred during the birth. Henry was said to be deeply grieved by the loss of Jane Seymour, but he chose to marry once again, this time to Anne of Cleves, on January 6th, 1540.

For whatever reason, this marriage did not seem to work out from the start. In July, the marriage was declared unconsummated and annulled. Henry was generous enough to give Anne a settlement and made sure her needs were taken care of. In truth, it could be that Henry simply decided he liked someone else better. Shortly after Anne was put aside, he married a woman named Catherine Howard, who had been in the direct employ of Anne's household.

But alas, this marriage would not last long and would end under even worse conditions since poor Catherine Howard was beheaded on charges of treason in 1542. This leads us to King Henry VIII's sixth and final wife: Catherine Parr. Henry wed Parr on July 12th, 1543, and the two remained married until Henry VIII's death in 1547.

Despite Henry VIII's volatile streak, Catherine Parr is said to have had a soothing effect and was able to reason with him where others could not. In fact, Catherine Parr managed to patch up the damaged relationship Henry had with his daughters, Mary and

Elizabeth, both of whom he had deemed illegitimate, making them unable to wear the crown. Catherine Parr convinced Henry to reinstate his daughters in the line of succession. This was made official by the Third Succession Act, which was passed in 1543.

This was smart thinking since his only son, Edward, would pass just a few years after taking the throne. King Edward VI perished on July 6th, 1553. Thanks to the Third Succession Act, Henry VIII's eldest daughter Mary, could be crowned queen, avoiding a potential civil war over the succession.

Henry VIII was ready to move heaven and earth to make sure he had a son on the throne. And yet, ultimately, his son's reign would be exceedingly brief, while his daughters would rule much longer. Despite all of the drama, intrigue, and six wives, his eldest child from his first marriage to Catherine of Aragon would sit on the throne.

Our story of the Tudors is not yet over, but before we dive into their stories, we will first take a look at one of the most earth-shattering events to happen in England: the English Reformation.

Chapter 4: England's Reformation Takes Shape

"The British do not expect happiness. I had the impression, all the time that I lived there, that they do not want to be happy; they want to be right."

-Quentin Crisp

The English Reformation was different than the one that had taken place in mainland Europe. Mainland Europe's Reformation, centered in the German-speaking lands, resulted from a doctrinal dispute with the Catholic Church. These disputes were centered around theology. There were arguments over everything, from the existence of purgatory to baptismal practices and how to take communion. But the biggest debate of all was over the sale of indulgences.

The Catholic Church had developed the belief that the pope had the authority to excommunicate parishioners if he felt it was necessary and lessen their time in purgatory. Catholics pointed to the words of Jesus when he declared to Peter (whom Catholics view as the first pope) that "whatever he binds on earth will be bound in heaven." Catholics took a literal interpretation of this, viewing the pope to be imbued with a binding authority. If he so decreed it, one's time in purgatory could be lessened.

As this belief developed, loved ones of the deceased petitioned the pope to lessen the deceased's time in purgatory. In time, this petition came to include an ample donation to the church. There is nothing too unusual about donating to churches; Catholic and Protestant churches alike still widely accept donations of all kinds. Churches would not be able to function and carry out good works, such as aiding the poor or building schools, if they did not receive contributions.

And it was very much the same during the Reformation. The pope was always commissioning building projects and needed money to finance them. This money often came through the sale of indulgences, which can be thought of as charitable donations with a catch (that catch being the papal promise of lessened time in purgatory in exchange for a donation).

The thing Martin Luther really seemed to take umbrage with was the sheer aggressiveness of the indulgence sellers. He was particularly disgusted by the way papal representatives went around poor villages in Europe hawking indulgences. There was even a famous catchphrase developed by a Catholic priest and contemporary of Luther named Johann Tetzel that went something along the lines of "As soon as a coin in the coffer rings, the soul from purgatory springs!" Corruption was rampant in the church as well; although donations were spent on building projects, much of it also went into church officials' pockets. It all became a bit too much for Martin Luther to stomach, and he would ultimately question the pope's supposed unbinding ability to lessen the time one might spend in purgatory.

Although there were those in England who disagreed with church doctrine, the main reason for England's breakaway from the church was not due to doctrinal disputes but rather the self-centered whims of England's monarch, Henry VIII. Despite his annoyance with the pope for not granting him an annulment, King Henry VIII was a dedicated Catholic. As such, his desire to break away from the church had nothing to do with religious doctrine and everything to do with deciding who would have authority over church matters.

Henry basically wanted to create his own mini replica of the Vatican in England so that he could preside over all of its happenings. Thus, the Church of England was designed to be a copy of the Catholic Church. Even so, some were itching to deviate from the path laid down by the Roman Catholic Church, and these proto-Protestants would soon come to the surface.

Major waves had been made by English Protestant William Tyndale back in 1526 when he successfully created an English translation of the Bible for everyday people to read. Prior to this, folks in England would have had to learn Latin just to read the scripture for themselves. Even more consequential was the fact that Tyndale translated his version directly from Hebrew and Greek sources, circumventing the Latin text altogether.

This created some subtle changes in the text, which outraged the Catholic Church. Tyndale was ultimately condemned, and Bishop Tunstall of London began a campaign of destroying Tyndale Bibles. And books were not the only things to be destroyed. Whoever was found with these condemned translations was likely to be prosecuted as well.

King Henry VIII's number one Catholic representative, the papal legate Thomas Wolsey, played an integral role when it came to punishing dissenters. Some of the most vicious campaigns against Protestants took place during the early 1530s, during which time Protestant dissenters were regularly burned at the stake for their religious views. Even while all of this was happening, King Henry VIII, frustrated with the pope's lack of cooperation with his marital affairs, decided to formally break away from the church.

Following Parliament's issuance of the Act of Supremacy in 1534, King Henry VIII was placed as the official head of England's church. Although Henry had denounced Martin Luther, who kicked off the Protestant Reformation, he ended up taking some cues from him in regard to the proto-nationalist notions that Luther had evoked. Luther, whether through pragmatic strategy or sincere belief, had always been able to pique the interest of heads of state by insisting they should have the final say over their nations rather than the pope in faraway Rome.

Henry could not help but agree, seeing that his annulment would never be officially sanctioned by the Catholic Church. Doctrinally, the Church of England was meant to be a clone of the Roman Catholic Church, but the severing of ties with papal authority would only encourage the strains of Protestant dissent to grow. During this time, many of England's previous stances were reversed. For example, Henry VIII sanctioned the translation of the Ten Commandments into English, a feat that would have previously been considered anathema.

The reversal would become even greater by 1538 when King Henry VIII began to call for a full English translation of the Bible itself. He would come to regret this decision, as once the lay public began to read the scripture for themselves, they could draw their own interpretation. Without official control over scripture and how it was presented to the masses, this would inevitably lead to different viewpoints. King Henry also feared that different interpretations would foment dissent against his authority.

In many ways, King Henry must have realized that he had shot himself in the foot. He had broken with the pope to ensure he had the final say in religious affairs but instead opened up Pandora's box. This Pandora's box unleashed a multitude of viewpoints and greatly increased the potential for dissent against his authority. Realizing as much, the incredibly frustrated King Henry VIII issued the Act for the Advancement of True Religion in 1543.

This act placed rules and regulations on who would be able to study scripture. Henry only wanted seasoned veteran preachers dedicated to the traditional views of the church reading the Bible, lest others develop contrary ideas of their own.

After Henry's passing, his son, Edward, came to the throne. Since Edward VI was still a child at the time, a regency council was put in place to stand for him until he came of age. The interesting thing about the king's counselors was that many of them were sympathizers of the Protestant cause. They and their associates had gleaned substantial benefits from seizing lands that had belonged to Catholic clergy. They realized that to maintain a monopoly over these benefits, they would have to make sure that England's new king continued to steer the nation away from Catholicism.

At this point in England's history, Protestants were still a minority. The Protestant movement was rapidly growing, but most people in England were faithful Catholics at this time. To have a council of Protestant-minded ministers tugging a young, impressionable king toward the Protestant cause meant that some deception likely took place. Thanks to Edward's ministers of state, the Act of Uniformity was passed by Parliament in 1549, which replaced the traditional Latin-based Mass with a uniform piece of liturgy called the *Book of Common Prayer.*

It was now the law of the land that prayers would be spoken in English rather than Latin. The new book provoked public outcry and even led to massive revolts in the cities of Devon and Cornwall, which would later be termed the Western Rebellion. King Edward died on July 6th, 1553, leaving much of his kingdom greatly divided over the Reformation. Upon his demise, the throne went to his half-sister, Princess Mary.

A portrait of Queen Mary I.
https://commons.wikimedia.org/wiki/File:Mary1_by_Eworth_3.jpg

To the delight of the Catholic faithful, Mary wished to return England back to the church. Protestant factions knew the writing was on the wall, as Mary was a staunch Catholic. They had attempted to prevent Mary's coronation. In fact, they tried to insert a prominent Protestant named Lady Jane Grey on the throne. Grey's claim to royalty was due to the fact that she was a great-granddaughter of Henry VII. On July 19th, 1553, Mary and her entourage swept into London and drove Grey and her supporters out.

Despite the fact that Mary would ultimately go down in history as a tyrant, at the time, she was supported by the majority of the public. Many felt some sense of relief when Lady Jane Grey, whom they viewed as an imposter being foisted upon them by the Protestant nobility, was removed and the rightful heir to the throne secured. Lady Jane Grey was ultimately arrested and put on trial for "high treason." She was found guilty as charged and executed on February 12th, 1554. She was seventeen years old.

It was not long before Mary turned her wrath on the Protestants of England, issuing bans on Protestant gatherings and arresting Protestant leaders. While she was locking Protestants up, Mary made an effort to release Catholic theologians who had been imprisoned during previous crackdowns. Understandably enough, the Catholic segment of England was happy with these developments, while the Protestant faction was miserable.

Making the Protestants of England even more upset was the news that Mary intended to wed the Catholic king of Spain, Philip II. Philip was not only the leader of one of the most powerful Catholic nations but also the son of Holy Roman Emperor Charles V, meaning he was the ruler of Spain and the scion of one of the most powerful men in Europe. The notion that England would be wed to such a formidable foreign power was viewed with incredible alarm. Even non-Protestants were on edge due to fears of what kind of foreign entanglement this union might bring for England.

Parliament spelled it out quite bluntly when a petition went out from the House of Commons that insisted Queen Mary should not wed a foreigner. Perhaps inheriting a bit of her father's stubborn streak, the queen refused to listen. Even after an armed insurrection broke out, she stood her ground. Her armies decimated the dissenters, and on July 25th, 1554, she married Philip II of Spain as planned.

This was welcome news to the pope. The Roman pontiff seemed to think England had sufficiently repented of its Protestant ways and issued a proclamation saying all had been forgiven and that England was welcomed back into the Catholic fold.

In England, life was good if you were a Catholic, but for those who still held onto some semblance of Protestant beliefs, they were in for some pretty brutal persecutions. In 1555, Queen Mary instituted heresy laws designed to punish and root out religious dissidents. This step led to the hunt of Protestants, who were then forced into unfair trials, with many being executed for their unwillingness to conform to the Catholic doctrine. Over three hundred Protestants were burned at the stake during this period, and many more were imprisoned. Due to this oppression, Queen Mary would forever become known as "Bloody Mary."

This nightmare would only come to an end when Mary passed on November 17th, 1558, succumbing to stomach cancer. After Mary's demise, Queen Elizabeth came to the throne. Elizabeth sided with the Protestants and paved the way for England to complete its Reformation that had technically begun under Henry VIII.

A portrait of Queen Elizabeth I.

Before we continue our story of the Tudors, it is worth taking a look at a historical figure that exemplifies the strife between Catholics and Protestants. Elizabeth I did not take the throne without some difficulties. Some called for Mary, Queen of Scots, to be the monarch of England. As the name implies, Mary was the monarch of Scotland, but she had a legitimate claim to the English throne, as she was the granddaughter of Margaret Tudor, the daughter of Henry VII. Mary, Queen of Scots, practiced Catholicism, and some were eager to bring England fully back into the Catholic fold.

However, history had other plans for Mary. Elizabeth was able to secure her rights to the throne, and Mary faced an uprising from her closest advisors. She was forced to abdicate, leaving the throne to her one-year-old son, James. Mary fled to England, hoping her cousin would take her in.

Elizabeth did take Mary in, but not the way she had anticipated. Mary, Queen of Scots, was imprisoned, although she still lived as her station afforded. She was not confined to some dreary cell in the Tower of London.

Alas, Mary's story does not end happily. After over eighteen years in captivity, Mary was sentenced to death due to her involvement in a plot to assassinate Elizabeth.

It is clear that England was ready for a Protestant queen since Mary's attempts to overthrow or assassinate Elizabeth never came to fruition. King Henry VIII had begun the process by cutting ties with Rome, while Edward, under the guidance of Protestant ministers, had furthered it along by reforming integral parts of church practice. Mary stood as the lone Tudor unwilling to move forward with church reforms, but her efforts failed. By the time of Elizabeth, there seemed to be no turning back the clock, and under her steady hand, the English Reformation would be complete.

Chapter 5: England and the Irish Question

"It's a mark of self-confidence: the English have not spent a great deal of time defining themselves because they haven't needed to."

-Jeremy Paxman

The question of what the ultimate fate of Ireland would be had loomed large in the minds of English rulers for centuries. In the last two years of Queen Mary's life, she established the first Irish plantations in the counties of Offaly and Laois. These plantations were essentially large tracts of land that were seized from the local Irish and then had English settlers transplanted onto them.

For all intents and purposes, this plantation strategy was the start of outright colonization of parts of the Irish homeland. English subjects were crowded in England and looking to expand. And considering this was before the Americas became the go-to place for colonists, the abundant lands of Ireland seemed like a natural enough destination. The Irish resented this encroachment. They disliked the seizure of land and found the insertion of what was fast becoming an increasingly alien culture intolerable.

Before the English Reformation, the Irish and English were often at odds with each other. But after the English Reformation, they were even further separated. The Irish remained staunchly Catholic, while the English began to accept Protestantism

---

wholeheartedly. King Henry VIII entreated Irish bishops to change their ways, but the Irish Catholic Church steadfastly refused.

By the time of Elizabeth, who came to the throne in 1558, there was an added religious element to the animosity between the Catholic Irish and the Protestant English, the latter of whom were newcomers to Ireland. The Irish were so alienated by the English that they often sided with foreign powers, as was the case in 1580 when rebellious Irish factions attempted to join forces with French and Spanish troops. This threat was defeated by England, but the potential for Ireland to become a backdoor to England's enemies remained.

This was demonstrated a few years later when the Spanish Armada sailed up the coasts of Ireland, hoping to hook up with Irish Catholic rebels. Due to logistical failures, bad weather, and the superior firepower of English ships, the Spanish fleet was ultimately repulsed. Nevertheless, the Irish would remain suspect in the eyes of many, including the famous Elizabethan poet Edward Spencer.

Spencer wrote the following rather unflattering words about the Irish: "Out of every corner of the woods and glens they came creeping forth upon their hands, for their legs could not bear them; they looked like anatomies of death, they spoke like ghosts crying out of their graves; they did eat of the dead carrions, happy were they could find them." Not exactly a resounding endorsement.

The Tudor dynasty ended up fighting four different wars against Ireland to get the Irish to submit to royal prerogatives. Even though the Irish held on to Catholicism, the campaigns waged by the English ruined much of the Irish way of life. The impact was felt the most keenly in Northern Ireland, especially in the region of Ulster.

The effect of English colonization can still be felt today, as most of the best real estate in Ulster is under the control of English Protestants, while the poorest, worst lands are the domains of Irish Catholics. The Anglicization of this region is painfully felt in the place names that have developed. In Ulster, we find a town that was once proudly called "Derry" transformed into

"Londonderry."

It is almost laughable in some ways, but, of course, there were many then, as there are now, who do not find this situation at all funny. But as it pertains to Ireland in the late 1500s, one of the biggest dissenters of the day was also perhaps one of the most unlikely: Grace O'Malley, the "Pirate Queen."

Grace O'Malley was the daughter of an Irish chieftain by the name of Owen Dubhdara O'Malley. Owen Dubhdara O'Malley was the leader of a self-governing principality in the patchwork of domains that made up Northern Ireland at the time. This situation began to change under King Henry VIII, who sought to divvy up some of the unincorporated lands of Ireland. Henry VIII instituted a policy of "surrender and regrant," in which he encouraged chieftains like Dubhdara to "surrender" themselves to the authority of the English monarchy. In turn, their lands would be officially "regranted" to them.

However, this meant the Irish chieftains would have to wash their hands of Irish law altogether and essentially be made an English earl who was subservient to the English monarch. Some chieftains were okay with this bargain and did as they were told, but there were others who refused. The animosity between those who complied and those who did not became downright intolerable, further dividing the social structure of Ireland.

Grace O'Malley's father was among those who refused to comply with the English call to submission. Grace grew up fast and strong. Although it was not common for women to take on leadership roles in those days, her strength of character helped propel her to a position of leadership among her people. During the frequent infighting among the various Irish clans, her husband, Dónal, was slain.

But Grace O'Malley proved her valor. She led a successful defense of the family castle, vanquishing her enemies. Shortly thereafter, Grace turned away from landed estates to the high seas. She acquired three galleys and recruited as many kinsfolk as possible to become her deckhands. This was the point when Grace O'Malley first became involved in piracy.

Grace certainly defied the social norms of her day. After her first husband's death, she unabashedly embarked upon a series of romances before remarrying a man named Richard Bourke in 1566. For other women, this would have damaged their reputation, but for Grace O'Malley, the Pirate Queen, it only added to her notoriety. One of the most infamous accounts of Grace on the high seas, which seems to fully encapsulate her "devil-may-care" attitude, occurred sometime in 1567 when her ship was intercepted by a Turkish pirate.

The Turks boarded the craft and were determined to take treasure and make the crew slaves. Grace was in bed when the Turks boarded the ship, having just birthed her son Theobald Bourke, also known as Tibbott-ne-Long. Any mother who has given birth can testify to how important rest and recovery are in the post-birthing process. But rest was not in the cards for Grace O'Malley.

As soon as she heard the ruckus taking place above deck, she rushed out of her cabin. With a gun in each hand, she leveled them at the Turks. She then made a statement that would go down in infamy: "Take this load from unconsecrated hands!"

O'Malley was referencing the old Catholic belief that women were "unconsecrated" or "unclean" after childbirth. It is unclear if Grace was making a mockery of the church, her assailants, her own situation, or perhaps all three, but she most certainly made an impression on her opponents.

They were actually so shocked by the sudden appearance of this infuriated Irish lady that they froze right in place. They just stood there while O'Malley fulfilled her pledge, unloading both barrels on the intruders. She killed multiple targets, and the rest ended up fleeing in terror.

At any rate, as it pertains to the so-called "Irish Question," you better believe that Grace O'Malley had plenty to say. And she would ultimately take her case directly to Queen Elizabeth herself. The year was 1593, and both Grace O'Malley, the Pirate Queen of Ireland, and Queen Elizabeth of England were well past their prime. Nevertheless, these two elder stateswomen sat down and had a frank, heart-to-heart discussion.

There were many matters to talk about. O'Malley's region of Ireland was being run by a tyrannical English governor named Richard Bingham. Various rebellions had broken out due to unrest, and O'Malley's son had been arrested for his part in the insurrection and was expected to hang. O'Malley spoke to the queen openly and honestly about her struggles, and the two eventually came to terms.

Queen Elizabeth agreed to fire Bingham as long as O'Malley pledged to cease and desist any further support of revolts in Ireland. Queen Elizabeth had compassion for O'Malley's rebel son and immediately issued an order to have him released from prison. For a time, Ireland was at peace. But fast forward to the year 1641, long after both O'Malley and Elizabeth were gone, and one would see that all hell was about to break loose.

That year, an all-out revolt erupted in Ireland, which saw the Irish attacking the Protestant English and Scottish settlers. In this major outbreak of violence, it is said that at least three thousand were slain. Most of the killings occurred in and around the region of Ulster. Making matters worse was the fact the current English monarch, Charles I, was married to a woman named Henrietta Maria, who was Catholic. This fact and other subsequent actions taken by the king would make others distrustful of him, especially those in his primarily Protestant Parliament.

There were rumors the king actually supported the uprisings in Ireland (or was at least sympathetic to them), and the Irish rebels were quick to monopolize this fact. The flames of discord were eventually fanned to such an extent that England erupted into a civil war. King Charles had to rush off to Nottingham, where he amassed troops loyal to his cause to prepare a march on Parliament.

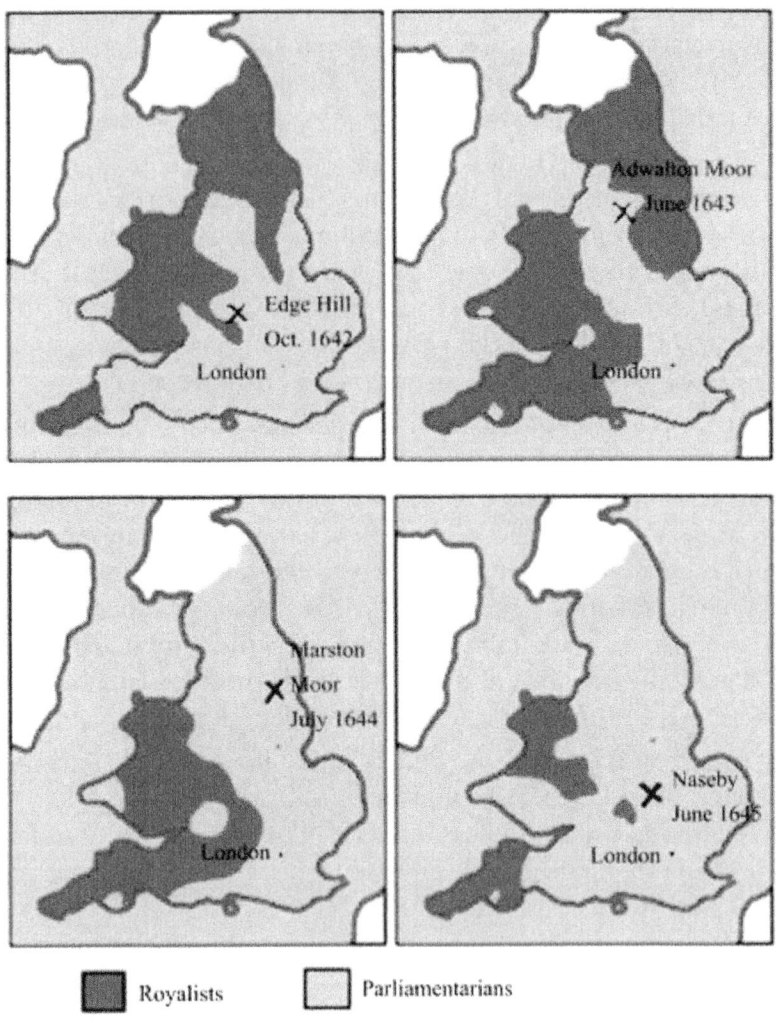

Royalists   Parliamentarians

Four maps that show the progression of the English Civil War. The top left shows the situation in 1642, while the bottom rights shows the territory held by the two sides in 1645.

The royalists made their stronghold in the northwestern parts of England, while the parliamentary forces secured the southeast. The royalist army quickly lost steam since bankrupt Charles found it difficult to pay them. Since King Charles's troops jumped ship in the droves, the royalist army was ultimately defeated in 1645, and Charles was forced to flee. He came back in 1648 to try and win the throne again but failed. Charles was executed in 1649; he was the only English monarch to be executed.

In the aftermath, the Parliamentarians had to figure out who would run England. A popular military commander named Oliver Cromwell ended up filling the gap, taking control in 1653 under the guise of "Lord Protector of England." Cromwell's reign was brief but eventful. Under his tenure, Jamaica was taken from Spain and made an English colony, and the Westminster Confession of Faith was declared as the prevailing doctrine of the Church of England. Cromwell was also involved in increasing the number of plantations in Ireland until he died in 1658.

Under Cromwell, land surveys in Ireland were conducted, and many of these territories were handed directly to Cromwell's loyal troops as a reward for their services. This led to many more plantations being established. Cromwell was just a mere flash in the pan, and two years after his death, the son of the deposed King Charles, Charles II, was welcomed onto the empty royal throne with open arms.

A portrait of King Charles II.
https://commons.wikimedia.org/wiki/File:Charles_II_by_John_Michael_Wright.jpg

The ramifications of the plantation system that had been foisted on Ireland would gravely impact the Irish. The effects of this system can still be felt to this day.

Chapter 6: Britannia Rules the World: The Empire

"The maxim of the British people is 'Business as usual.'"
-Sir Winston Churchill

It can be difficult to define the precise moment Britain became an empire. King Henry VIII first used the term, although he only oversaw England, Wales, and Ireland. During his high-profile struggle with the pope for an annulment, he issued the Statute in Restraint of Appeals in 1533, in which he solemnly stated, "This realm of England is an Empire."

Henry's wording was gauged more for effect than reality since he was attempting to portray himself as a sovereign emperor whose authority could not be overruled by the pope. At the time, one could hardly call England an empire since it had no real overseas colonies of which to speak. Instead of inserting themselves overseas, the English focused their energies on establishing plantations in Ireland.

This was, in many ways, a dress rehearsal for what would be done overseas. The first British colonies in the Americas came about in the early 1600s with some toeholds in the Caribbean. Its most important early settlement was Jamestown in what would one day become Virginia, a southeastern state in the United States.

The role Queen Elizabeth I played in the explorations of new lands and waters cannot be overstated. Elizabeth made England compete with Spain, opening the doors for further exploration by granting patents to explore new lands. She sent bold adventurers like Walter Raleigh to claim lands for England. Raleigh established a settlement on an island off North Carolina called Roanoke. This settlement would not last, but it set a precedent for more attempts.

After Queen Elizabeth I's passing in 1603, many of the initiatives she had begun would continue. The early settlements in the Americas would be followed by more extensive colonies that were built throughout the rest of the 17th century. As we mentioned in the previous chapter, this included the seizure of Jamaica from Spain in 1655.

England was so successful with its newfound colonies that Scotland tried to get in on it. In 1695, the Scottish launched the Darien scheme in which Scottish settlers landed on the Isthmus of Panama and established a fledgling colony. The colony struggled for a couple of years before it fell apart due to agitation from neighboring Spanish settlements and frequent outbreaks of sickness and disease.

Despite the fact the colony was a failure, it helped persuade Scotland and England to forge closer ties. England was horrified at the idea of Scotland exercising independent foreign policy in the Americas. At the same time, a greatly chastened Scotland had become more open to the idea of a merger so Scotland could partake of the benefits of England's growing empire. This led the two parties to agree to the Acts of Union of 1707. The United Kingdom of Great Britain was born.

Britain steadily expanded up the eastern seaboard of the United States, securing what would ultimately become the Thirteen Colonies. It was also making inroads into what would become Canada. However, the lands of Canada were already being actively settled by the French. It was almost inevitable these two nations would eventually butt heads.

Colonial competition between the two came to blows in the early 1700s, opening up a conflict in North America called Queen Anne's War, which began in 1702. It would not be until 1713 that the fighting would cease, thanks to the Peace of Utrecht. This treaty set clear boundaries between the British and the French in Canada. Britain acquired new lands in Newfoundland and Nova Scotia, allowing it to have a vast swath of territory that began in the uppermost reaches of Canada and ended just north of Florida, which at that time was still part of the Spanish Empire.

The Peace of Utrecht would keep the peace for the next few decades until the eruption of the French and Indian War. This war was part of a larger global conflict called the Seven Years' War. This war began in Europe after the hostilities unleashed from the tumultuous War of the Austrian Secession, which had Austria and Prussia at odds with each other and other European powers being forced to take sides.

Without getting too bogged down in the details of this complicated affair, just know that Britain and France ended up on opposing sides in the conflict. So, Britain and France began fighting each other in mainland Europe, and their battles quickly spilled over into their North American colonies as well. The American theater of this conflict is commonly known as the French and Indian War due to the fact that France had strong alliances with Native American tribes.

The French and their Native American allies fought against the British, who had some Native American tribes on their side as well. The British were ultimately able to defeat the French both on land and at sea, the latter of which played a crucial role due to the merciless bombardment unleashed by the British on French cities. France was forced to surrender in 1763, and the subsequent Treaty of Paris essentially handed over almost all French Canadian territories to the British. The British had a sprawling empire in just the Americas, but little did they know that they were about to lose a key part of it.

Just a little over a decade later, General George Washington, who had fought valiantly for the British during the French and Indian War, led American troops in a rebellion against the British. Ironically enough, the deep ramifications of the French and Indian War kicked off the American Revolution.

Although Britain was the victor of the French and Indian War, it was drained financially from all of the money it had expended to execute the war on multiple fronts. British authorities issued high taxes on the American colonies to recoup their losses. This exorbitant taxation created immense hostility in the Thirteen Colonies since locals had grown weary of suffering huge tax increases without even having a say in the matter. They had no formal representation in Parliament. This frustrating situation led to the popular outcry of "No taxation without representation!"

This frustration led to major protests, such as the Boston Tea Party in 1773, when Americans dressed up as Native Americans, made their way onto a ship loaded with tea, and proceeded to dump all of the tea into the harbor. They demonstrated their disgust at the high taxes on tea by dumping the goods rather than being forced to pay the taxes on them.

Typically, when the story of the American Revolution is told, the situation is presented in fairly cut-and-dry terms, presenting the Americans as well-defined dissidents and the British as well-defined oppressors. But, in truth, there were those in Britain who agreed with the colonists and wished to help them. Outspoken Parliament member John Wilkes is one of the most well-known examples. Wilkes may not have agreed with outright rebellion, but he was in lockstep with the notion that the colonists deserved better representation in Parliament.

If such voices encouraging reform had been heeded, there might not have been an American Revolution at all. But history did not play out that way. The voices calling for calm and constructive dialogue were eventually drowned out on both sides, and an all-out war erupted. The revolutionary struggle lasted from 1775 to 1783. In the end, Britain managed to hang on to Canada and its other overseas colonies, but it lost its Thirteen Colonies. A massive chunk had just been removed from the British Empire.

Nevertheless, Britain would soon gain ground on the other side of the world. Britain had already been involved in India through teams of traders and explorers, such as the British East India Company. Initially, relations between the British and the Indian population were fairly cordial. The British were just one of many competing powers wishing to do commerce and conduct business. It was not until the British began to seize Indian lands for themselves that this situation began to change.

In 1757, British troops took on the Mughal Empire, which controlled much of the Indian subcontinent, and seized the region of Bengal. The British gradually increased their territory from here on out. It inaugurated its very first governor-general of Bengal, Warren Hastings, in 1773, who rapidly consolidated British authority over its Indian territories.

Britain's next major milestone was when its old nemesis, France, was defeated in the Napoleonic Wars in 1815. With France out of the picture, Britain could really focus on empire-building in India and beyond. It is said that from 1815 to 1914 (sometimes called the "imperial century"), Britain added some ten million square miles and some four hundred million souls to its dominion.

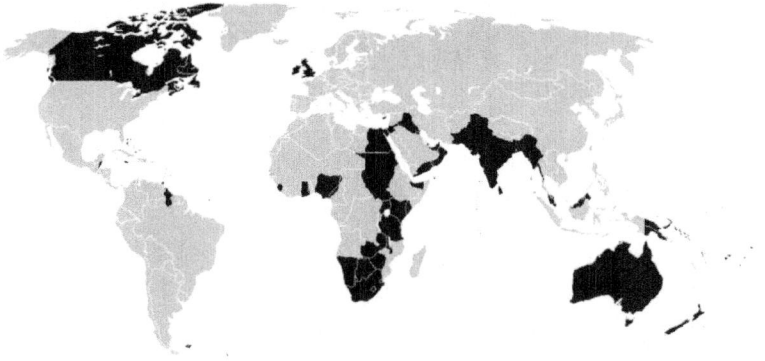

The British Empire in 1921.
https://commons.wikimedia.org/wiki/File:British_Empire_1921.png

Many criticize the British for "lording" over others, but the British did quite a bit of good along the way as well. They improved infrastructure in their colonies, encouraged education, and improved some aspects of civil society, which are rather benevolent acts for an occupying power. However, the British also took away lands from those who lived there, exploiting the land for raw materials and other goods. In some colonies, the people faced discrimination, poverty, and disease, and their former way of life was uprooted. For most, the jury is still out on whether it was good or bad that Britannia once ruled the world.

Chapter 7: Britannia and the World at War

"I think it's something to do with being British. We don't take
ourselves as seriously as other countries do."

-Joan Collins

It is interesting to note that the years 1815 to 1914 are often referred to as Britain's "imperial century," a century that is sandwiched between the end and the beginning of tremendous warfare. At the start of Britain's imperial century in 1815, Napoleonic France had just been defeated. This left the British Empire largely without a major antagonist for about one hundred years. Yet, in the final year of Britain's imperial century—1914— Britain would be dragged into a global war once again.

In 1914, the First World War erupted. As terrible as World War One was, it was sparked by an isolated incident. Archduke Franz Ferdinand was visiting Sarajevo in Bosnia when he was gunned down by a Serbian nationalist named Gavrilo Princip. It was a tragic episode, but it could have been handled without the world going to war. Yet, when it was learned that Princip had ties to a Serbian nationalist group, Austria-Hungary began making draconian demands.

Tensions between Austria-Hungary and Serbia were nothing new, and since Austria knew it had Serbia backed into a corner, it asked outrageous demands. When these demands were not met, Austria declared war on Serbia. This set off a chain reaction, as allied nations began declaring war on each other. Serbia's ally Russia declared war on Austria. Austria's ally Germany declared war on Russia. England and France were drawn into the fight, declaring war on Germany. Germany was aided by the Ottoman Empire, establishing the solid block of Central Powers that would take on the Allied forces of Serbia, Britain, France, Russia, and eventually the United States.

Germany, as centrally located as it is, had long feared being surrounded on all sides during a conflict. To prevent this, the German military implemented the Schlieffen Plan. This plan involved quickly mobilizing troops westward toward France in the hopes that France could be neutralized early in the war so that Germany's attention could be better focused on the Russian threat. The Schlieffen Plan called for going around the most heavily fortified parts of France by crossing through Holland, Belgium, and Luxembourg instead.

No one in the German high command really seemed to care these countries were neutral. For the German high command, steamrolling through these countries to get to the backdoor of France was just a means to an end. Initially, the Germans had the advantage and seemed poised to deal a knockout blow to the French, but the British Expeditionary Forces, who had just arrived on the scene, quite literally saved the day.

Aided by the British, the French lines held, and both sides dug in. The intense trench warfare resulted in a standoff, which would characterize the Western Front for most of the war. Each side tried to make inroads against the other, but for the most part, gains would be minimal, and losses would be great.

This was the case during a British-led offensive in 1915 that had the British and French slamming into German positions near the towns of Champagne and Artois. The Allies tried their best to break through the German positions, but in the end, they were pushed back by machine gun fire with nothing to show for their efforts but a great loss of life.

In the meantime, the Germans decided to take the fight to the British homeland itself. They did this by floating air-filled

Zeppelins (a type of airship) over the skies of London. Once in place, these Zeppelins dropped incendiary explosives on the city.

Although the Zeppelins did not drop bombs accurately on their targets, they did a lot of damage and killed several people. Interestingly enough, the leader of Germany, Kaiser Wilhelm II, was initially against using Zeppelins in this manner, citing his fear that they might obliterate much of "London's cultural heritage." The Kaiser was eventually overruled by his generals, though.

For the people of Britain, it must have been truly a terrible sight to witness these behemoths suddenly appear on the horizon. But Britain was not completely defenseless against these airborne monsters. Once the proper combination of searchlights and powerful artillery were in place, it was quite easy for them to knock these airships out of the sky. All they had to do was light up the target and let loose with their artillery. Just one hit and the Zeppelin would crumble. The Royal Air Force also got in on the action, and British fighter craft were soon making short work of the German Zeppelins.

Although the main focus of the war was on the Western Front, an incredibly consequential theater of conflict for both Britain and the world was being engaged in Asia Minor or, as we call it today, Turkey.

During World War One, Turkey was the seat of the Ottoman Empire, which at that time still controlled much of the Middle East and North Africa. Since the Ottoman Empire aligned itself with the other Central Powers (Austria-Hungary and Germany), it was automatically the enemy of Britain. Intense fighting took place when British troops landed on the Gallipoli Peninsula in mainland Turkey and participated in the subsequent Battle of Gallipoli.

The battle was a miserable failure for the British. Due to poor planning and logistical problems, British troops ended up stuck on the peninsula for several months, fighting a bloody stalemate against ferocious Turkish troops before the Allies retreated. Although the Ottoman Empire and the other Central Powers were defeated in the end, the Ottoman troops put up an effective front in the Battle of Gallipoli.

The next time the Ottoman Turks would face off against the British in a major way would be in what has been dubbed the

Battle of Armageddon. Taking place in the ancient Israeli fields of Tel Megiddo, the lines were once again drawn between the Turks and the British. This battle was actually a series of battles, which are numbered from the First Battle of Gaza to the Third Battle of Gaza. During the Third Battle of Gaza, the British managed to make an offensive drive into the Turkish positions at Beersheba.

To the delight of Britain's crusader past, the British fought all the way to Jerusalem itself. These developments led to the famous scene of British General Edmund Allenby making his way into Jerusalem in December 1917. This event would have huge ramifications for the entire world. The Ottomans would ultimately be defeated, and the region of Israel/Palestine, which had been under the Ottoman administration for hundreds of years, would be placed under a British mandate.

The British would control the region for the next few decades. After World War Two, in 1948, the United Nations recognized the state of Israel.

At any rate, in World War I, the Allies would be victorious on all fronts, and the Central Powers of Austria-Hungary, Germany, and the Ottoman Empire would be defeated. Austria-Hungary and the Ottoman Empire were broken up.

The end of the war created new nation-states or saw the emergence of independent states in the Balkans, the Middle East, and North Africa. Some territories would end up under the control of other powers. For example, Japan, which fought with the Allies during World War One, received much of Germany's extra-territorial holdings in Asia.

Germany faced the most severe financial and military restrictions. The Treaty of Versailles, which signaled the end of the war, impacted Germany by demanding severe reparations and significantly curtailing its military. Many Germans resented this. By the time Adolf Hitler rose to power in the 1930s, they were openly applauding his pledge to rip up the treaty, stop paying reparations, build up the German military, and retake lost territory.

Although there is a multitude of factors involved in the lead-up to World War II, the harsh terms of the Treaty of Versailles certainly played a large role. Britain took center stage during much of Germany's saber-rattling in the 1930s. The British attempted to appease and prevent aggressive German behavior from sparking another world war. The British public largely had no appetite for war, and British Prime Minister Neville Chamberlain's efforts to keep Britain from becoming embroiled in a war with Germany over faraway territorial disputes were viewed as pragmatic.

But when Hitler overplayed his hand and invaded Poland in 1939, even Neville Chamberlain's pragmatic patience ran out. At this point, Britain and France declared war on Germany. Germany declared war right back.

At first, the Allies did very little besides issue a blockade and feverishly rearm their militaries. By 1940, Britain had turned its attention toward Norway and Sweden, which was where Germany imported its iron ore. Plans were made to seize these ore deposits by force. The Germans beat the Allies to it and launched an invasion of Norway that spring. The Allies attempted to send a relief force to Norway, but the Germans seized control of the country so rapidly that the Allied efforts were deemed futile. As a result, the British pulled back. The next thing anyone knew, German tanks were racing into France that summer.

In a virtual repeat of the Schieffelin Plan, Hitler was determined to drive through the Low Countries of Belgium, Holland, and Luxembourg so that France could be quickly knocked out of the war. Unfortunately for France, this time around, the offensive worked. France was overwhelmed in the face of the blitzkrieg unleashed upon it and forced to surrender.

Those British still fighting this apparently lost cause in France were forced to engage in a rearguard fighting action as they retreated back to the beachhead of the small port of Dunkirk. Here, the British valiantly fought off the Germans so that their troops could be evacuated. Many were ferried across the English Channel in privately owned ships.

It was an impromptu escape from mainland Europe, but it worked and prevented a good chunk of the British army from being destroyed. The newly installed British Prime Minister Winston Churchill latched onto this moment and declared it a demonstration of "courage and determination at Britain's darkest hour."

Churchill went on to speak before his fellow legislators and declared, "We shall defend our island, whatever the cost may be, we shall fight on the beaches, we shall fight on the landing grounds, we shall fight in the fields and in the streets, we shall fight on the hills; we shall never surrender."

Shortly thereafter, the Royal Air Force engaged in what has become known as the Battle of Britain. In this struggle, British fighter planes squared off against German fighter planes as both struggled to gain dominance over Britain's skies. After three months of engaging each other, the British managed to come out on top. This was important since Germany intended to knock out Britain's air force and then launch an outright invasion.

The German invasion, codenamed Operation Sea Lion, was unable to take place because of the Royal Air Force's fierce resistance. But even though these plans were thwarted, German planes continued to conduct nightly bombing raids that would later be referred to as the Blitz. Despite the odds, Britain was able to hang on, and thanks to two misguided attacks launched by the Axis Powers of Germany and Japan, two of the world's most powerful militaries would soon be fighting on its side.

First, Germany invaded the Soviet Union, sending Russia into the Allied camp. And then, Japan attacked the United States, bringing America's might and industry on the side of Britain as well. By 1943, Russia was driving Germany back from eastern Europe. The third member of the Axis Powers, Italy, surrendered that year. In 1944, US and British troops landed in western Europe.

In May 1945, Germany surrendered, and in September of that same year, Japan surrendered as well. Britain had seen the war through to its end and helped lead it to a successful conclusion. But the British Empire of old was on life support and would soon be dismantled entirely.

PART TWO: Scotland, Wales, and Northern Ireland

Chapter 8: Scotland: A Tale of Three Williams and a Glorious Revolution

"There's an accent shift, on average, every 25 miles in England."
-David Crystal

Scotland stands as a majestic and enchanting land. None other than the famed bard William Shakespeare captured the essence of Scotland best. To be sure, Shakespeare himself was English through and through, but his masterpiece play *Macbeth* gives us a great window into what the Scotland of old must have been like.

In order to understand Shakespeare's tale, one must know a little bit about the backdrop that inspired him. From his perch in the 1600s, William Shakespeare cast his mind back centuries into Scotland's past when Scottish warlords battled for dominance. Norse incursions were common during this period, adding yet another layer of complexity to the landscape.

Shakespeare's *Macbeth* took place in the 11th century in the wild northern reaches of Scotland's interior. The main character, Macbeth, was a real Scottish king who reigned from 1040 to 1057. In the play, Macbeth gets wrapped up in typical royal intrigue and finds himself compelled to resort to murder to stay in power.

The real Macbeth was King Macbeth mac Findlaech. Macbeth's grandfather was King Malcolm of Scotland; after Malcolm's passing, his grandson, Duncan, became king. Duncan would become entangled with Norse warriors who infiltrated Britain and ended up embroiled in hostilities with England.

Even though Shakespeare murders Duncan in his play, the real Duncan actually perished on the battlefield. Another myth was Shakespeare's portrayal of Macbeth as a neurotic, impulsive ruler who could be quickly disposed of. The real-life Macbeth was quite decisive and remained in power for seventeen years. In the end, Macbeth was taken out by Duncan's son, Malcolm III Canmore.

Fast forward one hundred years from Macbeth's death, and another famous William emerges (this time, one from Scotland): William Wallace. William Wallace came to prominence at a time when Scotland was being severely oppressed by the English Crown. Scotland had just faced a succession crisis after its king died without an immediate heir, leading to the establishment of the Guardians of the Kingdom of Scotland.

Initially, the Guardians shepherded the dead king's granddaughter. The hope was that Margaret, the "Maid of Norway," would one day lead Scotland. But this slim hope was lost when she perished in 1290. Scotland was in some really dire straits, as various factions began to throw their weight around in their bid to lead.

In this tense atmosphere, King Edward I of England was invited to help broker a successor. In the end, John Balliol was chosen. However, Balliol would ultimately be viewed as nothing more than a puppet of the English king who helped bring him to power. He earned the nickname "Toom Tabard," which means "Empty Coat."

The Scottish public began to groan under this oppressive proxy of England, and William Wallace was one of them. Wallace was particularly disgusted with the occupying English forces who had taken up root ever since Toom Tabard had been installed on the throne. Thus, Wallace began to strike out against the occupiers. It is not clear how much of these early tales are accurate, but it is said that he engaged in a few hit-and-run attacks on troops stationed in the region.

However, his real vendetta began immediately after he was accosted by English troops as he was leaving a local church. Wallace was apparently minding his own business when a foul-mouthed soldier began hassling him in a very personal manner. In the close-knit community of which Wallace was a part, personal details were typically well known. Wallace had just wed a lady named Marion Braidflute, and this lout apparently knew all about it.

The troublemaking soldier took one look at Wallace, whose belt was adorned with a fine dagger on his side, and howled, "What should a Scot do with so fair a knife—as the priest said who last f***** your wife!" The words were obviously meant to provoke William Wallace, but since he had only a handful of friends with him compared to the large number of English troops who stood in the street, he knew he would be no match.

As such, Wallace attempted to ignore the vile jibes thrown at him. The troops would not stop, and Wallace finally snapped. Erupting in pure fury, he unleashed his blade, taking out several of the hecklers. Thanks to the narrow, winding streets, he was able to cut his way to freedom, leaving his enemies slipping and sliding in the puddles of blood congealing under their feet.

It is ironic that a narrow passage saved him during this melee since years later, at his most famous moment as a Scottish rebel leader, the narrowness of a bridge doomed his antagonists. The tactic used in the Battle of Stirling Bridge was simple but stunningly effective. Wallace and his men were on one side of the bridge, while the larger English army sent to subdue them was on the other side.

Wallace goaded the English into crossing the bridge. The English were then immediately bottlenecked, forced to march in no more than two columns. As the English emerged two by two on the other side, it was quite easy for Wallace and his rebels to waylay them. The English were decimated in "pairs." Two would emerge from the bridge, only to get hacked to pieces by the full force of Wallace's rebels. Almost the entire English entourage was decimated before the remnant that survived finally realized their mistake and fled in retreat.

Regardless of his great triumph at Stirling Bridge, William Wallace, the great Scottish freedom fighter, was eventually defeated and captured. On August 23rd, 1305, he was executed in just about as horrific a manner as anyone could imagine. Stripped of his clothes, he was literally dragged through the streets naked before he was forced up to the hangman's gallows. The noose was placed around his neck, and he was dropped, hanging from a rope. However, just before he was about to expire, the executioner cut the rope.

Unbelievably, the semi-conscious Wallace then had his genitals cut off. This was most certainly painful enough to bring Wallace to a fully conscious state. And as he screamed in horror, William Wallace's belly was sliced apart and his bowels extracted. His entrails were set on fire and burned in front of his own eyes. Wallace lived through all of this and only perished when his heart was literally torn from his chest.

Even after he was dead, the abuse continued. He was decapitated, and his body was chopped into four pieces. Each limb was severed, with a hunk of gory flesh still attached. William Wallace's fate presents us with a tale too terrible for even the darkest of Shakespearean dramas to imagine.

A statue of William Wallace.

A few decades after the end of Shakespeare's life, there was more than enough drama going on in Scotland. The Glorious Revolution, which took place in 1688, revolved around the dual monarch King James, who was known as King James II of England and Ireland, as well as King James VII of Scotland.

In what was essentially a simultaneous external invasion and internal coup, William III of Orange invaded Britain, while ministers ousted the king of England in favor of his daughter and William's wife, Mary II. All of this drama centered around the fact that James was Catholic. Although he was somewhat popular when he first sat on the throne, his policies quickly grated on the nerves of the Protestant majority of England.

For this reason, many began looking toward his Protestant daughter Mary as a potential alternative. Mary was the release valve for the anxieties of many since they believed Mary would soon sit on the throne rather than her Catholic father. Mary was also married to William of Orange, a Protestant cousin who administered the Dutch Republic. However, these plans were disturbed when King James unexpectedly sired a son named James Francis Edward.

This was unexpected since James's wife was in her forties at the time. Little James Francis Edward was born to King James and his wife, Mary of Modena, on June 10th, 1688. Due to the laws of succession, a male heir automatically superseded a female heir, placing baby James as the immediate heir apparent. The birth of this new heir set in motion the plot to get rid of King James.

Young James disturbed King James's opponents because they knew the boy would likely be raised in the Catholic faith. As infighting continued to grow, James's opponents actually "invited" William of Orange to come to England to stage an intervention. On November 5th, 1688, William of Orange landed in force.

Just before William's landing, a supporter of King James in Scotland, one Viscount Dundee John Graham of Claverhouse, otherwise known as "Bloody Clavers," was prepared to support his Scottish royal brethren by gathering an army of some thirteen thousand warriors. As the situation grew increasingly tense, he prepared to send them south to serve as a vanguard for King James.

For those in the king's immediate circle, the situation looked increasingly untenable. Even this large militia would be of little help, considering they were facing the forces of the Duke of Orange. Fearing the worst, the queen and the young heir were quietly evacuated on December 9th. Apparently not taking much stock in Bloody Clavers's support, King James himself went into exile on December 23rd, 1688.

Perhaps the reason this revolution is considered so "glorious" is that it was essentially bloodless. No one was willing to fight for King James in the end. That April, Protestant Mary was made queen by the Protestant-leaning Parliament members. And not only that but William was also made king in an arrangement that gave England joint monarchs.

The coronation of William and Mary.
https://commons.wikimedia.org/wiki/File:SA_4973-Anno_1689._De_kroning_van_Willem_III_en_Maria_Stuart.jpg

That spring, the Parliament went a step further to ensure its Protestant dominance would continue. In February 1689, the Act of Settlement was put forth, which banned any Catholics from sitting on the throne. Today, we would no doubt flinch at such discriminatory practices, but the Protestant Parliamentarians certainly had their reasons.

Britain had lived through several centuries of turmoil due to the conflict between Protestants and Catholics, and the Protestant majority simply wanted to ensure the matter was finally "settled" and that there would not be a sudden return to a Catholic monarchy, which might upset the status quo. We can see what happened when the status quo was upset when Henry VIII's staunchly Catholic daughter Mary took the throne and attempted to reverse just about every Protestant-based law in the books.

With the Act of Settlement, the Protestants considered the matter settled and insisted that in the future, only Protestant kings and queens would rule England. Despite the religious overtones, this was a major milestone in the transformation of England into a constitutional monarchy. The Parliament had an active say in not only how the monarch ran the country but also over who could even be king or queen in the first place.

As it pertains to the Glorious Revolution, we have not quite reached the end of the story. In the fateful summer of 1689, Viscount Dundee sent his troops, who came to be known as Jacobites (Latin for James), down the slopes of Killiecrankie in the vicinity of Blair Atholl. He did so with the intention of leading a belated counterrevolution of his own, referred to as the Jacobite uprising.

Viscount Dundee led the charge, and upon making contact with the opposition, he was pounded in the head with a musket shot and perished shortly after that. After Dundee's death, the struggle would continue until May 1690, but nothing would be able to undo what the Glorious Revolution had begun. The end result served to confirm the status quo in regard to Protestants and Catholics in Scotland.

Chapter 9: A Brief Guide to Welsh History

"To be born in Wales, not with a silver spoon in your mouth, but, with music in your blood and with poetry in your soul, is a privilege indeed."

-Brian Harris

Wales has a long history of settlement that can be traced back to the earliest epochs of prehistory. The region first entered into the historical record around 48 CE when Romans came to the region to make it part of the Roman Empire. Wales would remain under Roman dominion all the way until 383. By the time the Romans had left, Wales had greatly changed. Most were Christian and set about to create a patchwork of independent kingdoms.

The Welsh chieftains would periodically come to blows with their neighbors, the Anglo-Saxons, but the Anglo-Saxons did not have the wherewithal to defeat the Welsh outright. They did continuously encroach upon the borderlands they shared with Wales, though. In the meantime, the Welsh continued to fight amongst each other, with various warlords vying for power.

Wales was not truly united under one ruler until Gruffydd ap Llywelyn came to power in 1055. Anyone who takes a momentary glance at Scottish history will notice the curious phenomenon of rulers with "ap" as their middle name. Although "ap" is most likely going to make the modern-day person think of a software application on their smartphone, back in Wales, "ap" was merely a Welsh word for "son of."

It was a Welsh tradition to recognize fathers by utilizing their first name as one's last name. For instance, if your name was John and your father was Bob, you would be dubbed John, son of Bob, or John "ap" Bob. And the "son of" lineage would carry on down the family line from there. As it pertains to Gruffydd ap Llywelyn, he was the son of a previous powerful Welsh ruler named Llywelyn ap Seisyll.

Gruffydd rose to prominence by killing or gaining compliance from any potential rivals. He became the first Welsh king to lead over a truly united kingdom (not to be confused with *the* United Kingdom). Not only that, but Gruffydd ap Llywelyn was also able to expand out of Wales and seize parts that the Anglo-Saxons had previously held. The Welsh would never again be on the offensive like they were under this dynamic Welsh king. He ultimately perished in 1063, leaving a power vacuum in his wake.

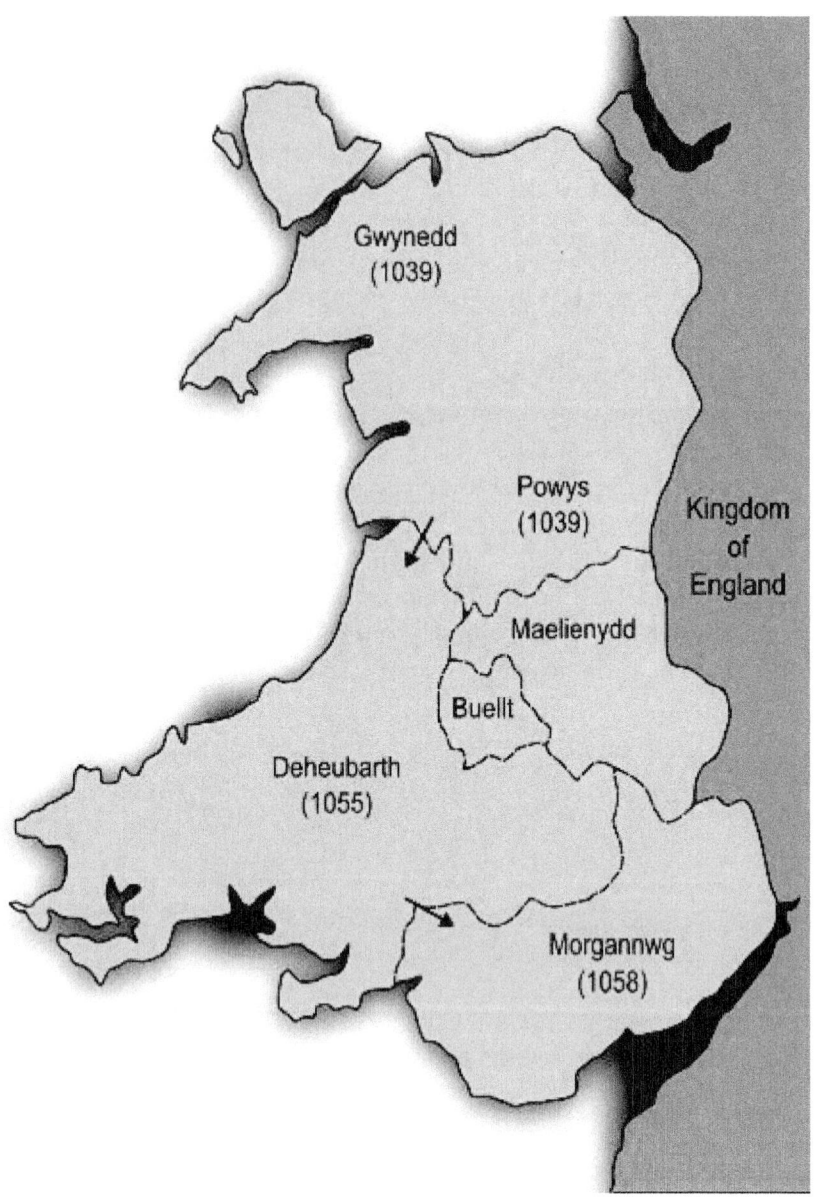

Map of Gruffydd ap Llywelyn's conquests.

By the time of the Norman invasion in 1066, the situation in Wales was unstable, and the Normans rampaged through the Welsh region of Deheubarth. William the Conqueror eventually led his troops into Dyfed and set up many fortresses. The Welsh were finally able to regroup and push back, and in 1094, many of the previously lost lands were regained. The death knell for the Normans in Wales occurred over a hundred years later in 1136 when the Norman forces were crushed at the Battle of Crug Mawr.

Led by the valiant Welsh leader Owain Gwynedd, this engagement settled the matter for good, at least as far as the Normans were concerned. But it would not be the end of attempts to colonize Wales. King Edward I of England would ultimately subdue Wales. In the summer of 1277, the armies of King Edward were sent into Wales for a final confrontation.

By this time, the Welsh were just a shadow of what they had been. They had been greatly reduced in number, and the sitting Welsh ruler—Llywelyn ap Gruffudd—was forced to hole up with what few troops he had and prepare for a long siege in his fortress at Gwynedd. At this point, even the fiery Llywelyn could not help but see the writing on the wall and sued for peace, which led to the Treaty of Aberconwy. The treaty reduced the Welsh ruler's kingdom to nothing more than Gwynedd itself.

However, the treaty would not last, and Edward launched another invasion in the spring of 1283. This spelled the end of Welsh independence and led to Edward taking the title of prince of Wales. The title is still held by the royal family to this day. The title goes to the next in line for the throne; with Queen Elizabeth's passing, the title now belongs to her grandson, Prince William.

From this point forward, Wales would essentially be a territory of the Crown but would not be officially a part of the kingdom until the issuance of the Laws in Wales Acts, which were a series of laws passed from 1535 to 1542.

Despite their subjugation at the hands of the English, the Welsh had long been passionate about their independence. They desired to hold on to their lands, but even when that was taken from them, they continued to celebrate their culture and way of life. Much of Welsh literature plays into this, with literary figures held up as heroic figures who may one day reclaim the glory of the Welsh past. Probably no other Welsh literary character fulfills this role better than King Arthur.

Some might be surprised to hear Arthur is associated with Wales, as in later years, the legendary King Arthur and his Round Table were thoroughly Anglicized. But the tales of King Arthur are indeed Welsh in origin. The first mention of Arthur can be traced back to a Welsh cleric whose name comes down to us as Nennius. From the writings of Nennius, the *Historia Brittonum* (*The History of the Britons*) was put together in the 9th century.

This work describes Arthur as a great leader who fought in twelve major battles, the greatest of which was the legendary Battle of Badon, where Arthur allegedly decimated 960 enemy troops with his own hands. Such things are hard to entertain from a historical perspective, but it is from these legendary tales that the notion of a great and powerful king named Arthur first entered the medieval consciousness.

Along with Arthur came the Welsh figure of Merlin. As anyone who has read Arthurian mythology will know, Merlin was King Arthur's mentor and guide. He was also a magician and visionary mystic who not only had things to say during Arthur's lifetime but also allegedly spouted prophecies for the future of Wales. After the Welsh were overrun by the English, some of these prophetic folktales came to prominence as the last hope of an oppressed people.

In the *Historia Brittonum*, we get a glimpse of Merlin's origin story. Before his story became Anglicized, the Welsh name for Merlin was actually Myrddin, which roughly translates as "mad man." Myrddin is said to have been a mystic who lived by himself in the rugged Welsh highlands of Snowdonia. Here, he had a vision of the future of Wales, which was represented by two dragons. He saw a red dragon locked in combat with a white dragon. It was a terrific struggle, but ultimately, the red dragon was triumphant and forced the white dragon to flee.

Merlin (Myrddin) understood the red dragon to be Wales and the white dragon to be England. According to Merlin's prophecy, Wales would triumph over England one day. After England conquered Wales, any talk of this prophecy was strictly forbidden. English authorities feared these tales would inspire future revolts and rebellions from their Welsh subjects.

Many of the Arthurian legends were coopted by the English, both in order to make the tales more palpable for a wider English audience and to muffle and mute the revolutionary and nationalistic overtones of the narrative. King Edward I, who had much to do with the final subjugation of Wales, even went as far as to create an elaborate hoax, claiming that King Arthur's tomb had been found in Glastonbury. This was done to prove that the great Welsh king was dead and accounted for rather than living in exile in the magical land of Avalon, waiting to one day return as the original Welsh mythology foretold.

English kings did not want the Welsh to think their hero was about to swoop down from Avalon and lead them to freedom. They sought to bury the story by claiming they had the buried bones of Arthur in their possession. Although England made great efforts to bury the Welsh language, culture, and traditions, the Welsh refused to give in. Calls for independence can be heard throughout Wales today. In January 2021, a survey was taken to see if the Welsh would be interested in holding a referendum on Welsh independence. Although 47 percent voted no, 31 percent voted yes, which was a major increase from past surveys.

Chapter 10: The Time of Troubles in Northern Ireland

"There are two traditions in Northern Ireland. There are two main religious denominations. But there is only one true moral denomination. And it wants peace."

-David Trimble

Northern Ireland has always been a point of contention in the British Isles, but it was not until the 1920 Government of Ireland Act that the boundaries of Northern Ireland were drawn. This act effectively divided Ireland into two self-governing regions: the Republic of Ireland and Northern Ireland. The Republic of Ireland would still be part of Britain, breaking away from the British Commonwealth in 1948. Today, Northern Ireland is still part of the United Kingdom. Under the Government of Ireland Act, Northern Ireland consisted of six counties and would be governed from the city of Belfast.

The six counties of Northern Ireland.

Maximilian Dörrbecker (Chumwa), CC BY-SA 2.5
<https://creativecommons.org/licenses/by-sa/2.5>, via Wikimedia Commons;
https://commons.wikimedia.org/wiki/File:Northern_Ireland_-_Counties.png

Northern Ireland, as a separate entity, was officially established on May 3rd, 1921. However, not everyone agreed with this arrangement, and Protestant unionists and Catholic separatists duked it out in the streets. This massive unrest would become known as "the Troubles."

The main flashpoint was the province of Ulster, which was predominantly Protestant. All of the government positions in Ulster were controlled by Protestants, and Catholics were consistently blocked from taking up positions of authority. In some instances, they were even prevented from voting. And it was not only in Ulster that these problems were occurring; there was an instance in Belfast in 1920 when Irish Catholics and Irish Protestants erupted in terrible violence at a Belfast shipyard. The following year saw the infamous Belfast's Bloody Sunday, in which at least twenty lost their lives.

Belfast's Bloody Sunday occurred on July 10th, 1921, on the heels of a brokered ceasefire between the Irish Republican Army (IRA) and British authorities. Just hours prior to the start of the ceasefire, the British authorities decided to raid IRA compounds in West Belfast. While British police were doing this, they were suddenly attacked by IRA fighters. In the immediate exchange, one British cop was killed, and several others were injured.

The outbreak of fighting sparked several simultaneous outbursts of violence all throughout Northern Ireland. Before it was all said and done, at least twenty people would be dead, and hundreds of properties would be vandalized. In the aftermath of this bloodshed, the Anglo-Irish Treaty was signed on December 6th, 1921. This treaty established the Irish Free State.

The Irish Free State encompassed twenty-six of the thirty-two Irish counties, with Northern Ireland making up the six that were not part of the free state. The terms of the treaty declared that Northern Ireland could eventually be incorporated into the Irish Free State if it so desired, or it could choose to opt out permanently by petitioning the British monarch. This led to a meeting of the Parliament of Northern Ireland on December 7th, 1922, where a direct address was made to King George V.

The declaration stated, "Most Gracious Sovereign, We, your Majesty's most dutiful and loyal subjects, the Senators and Commons of Northern Ireland in Parliament assembled, having learnt of the passing of the Irish Free State Constitution Act 1922, being the Act of Parliament for the ratification of the Articles of Agreement for a Treaty between Great Britain and Ireland, do by this humble address, pray your Majesty that the powers of the Parliament and Government of the Irish Free State shall no longer extend to Northern Ireland."

Thereafter, it was incumbent upon the Irish Boundary Commission to set up the proposed border between the Irish Free State and Northern Ireland. This was easier said than done since there were endless squabbles about where the border would be. The infighting was so terrible that this task was not accomplished until 1925. The fighting would continue sporadically for much of the rest of the 20th century, with some of the worst instances of bloodshed happening in the 1960s and 1970s.

Known as the Troubles, the fighting would not cease entirely until the 1990s. During this period of intense violence, it is estimated that some 3,254 people lost their lives, not to mention the tens of thousands who were horrifically injured. Street fighting erupted on nearly every corner, and random bombings became all too common.

Despite the bloodshed, the Irish Catholics of Northern Ireland insisted they were merely fighting for a fair shake. Northern Ireland was mostly Catholic and argued it wanted equal representation in the Protestant-led government. In addition, there were groups that wanted to form a united Ireland and called for separation from Britain. Some groups, like the IRA (Provisional Irish Republican Army), used terrorism to spread their message.

From 1967 to 1972, the Northern Ireland Civil Rights Association fought to put a stop to alleged discrimination and disenfranchisement of Catholics. But rather than achieving civil reform, this Irish civil rights movement sparked intense backlash, and terrible violence once again erupted, this time led by paramilitary groups.

The situation became so bad that in 1972, the autonomous regional government of Northern Ireland was shut down and suspended. Peace was eventually restored, but it was a slow process. First of all, efforts had to be made to convince the paramilitary groups to stand down.

After intense negotiation, ceasefires were declared by almost all of the paramilitary fighters, and their weapons were seized. Next, the police were significantly reformed, and British troops were pulled from the hot spots. It has been a long, drawn-out process, but today, Northern Ireland is largely at peace.

However, due to recent developments, there are those who fear there could be a modern-day resurgence in violence. In recent years, there has been a noticeable uptick among young people interested in the hardline stances of the IRA past. There is an increase in nationalism and sentiments of isolationism.

Recently, the ultra-nationalist Irish political group known as Sinn Féin, whose name means "We Ourselves," has gained traction in Northern Ireland. Sinn Féin holds out the promise of allowing the Irish to be, well, Irish, or at least their interpretation of what it means to be Irish. And while there is certainly nothing wrong with a nation wishing to celebrate its culture and heritage, it is indeed troubling to many to see Sinn Féin come to prominence since they had such strong ties with the IRA during the darker periods of Northern Ireland's turbulent past.

Sinn Féin managed to stun the world by winning a huge share of votes in the 2022 election, marking the first time such a hardline nationalist group in Ireland has come to such prominence. As of this writing, Sinn Féin, led by Irish firebrand Mary Lou McDonald, now holds seven seats in the United Kingdom's House of Commons. Is Ireland headed back to the dark days of the Troubles? Or will this new embrace of Sinn Féin and Irish populism somehow lead to something better? Only time will tell how this might affect Britain.

Conclusion: In Consideration of Britain

Britain entered history as a wild and untamed island on the fringes of "civilized" Roman society. Roman greats, such as Julius Caesar, attempted to tame the isle and took on its Celtic inhabitants, resulting in climatic battles. In the end, the best the Romans could do was subdue a large chunk of England and seal it off with a wall, courtesy of Roman Emperor Hadrian.

As Europe entered the Dark Ages, Britain was swarmed by Germanic tribes, who became to be known as the Anglo-Saxons. They coopted and contributed to the Roman framework that was already in place. In time, many of these newcomers became Christians and adopted Roman legal practices as they set about establishing kingdoms of their own.

The Anglo-Saxons faced very little opposition and set about establishing the boundaries of what would become modern-day England. In the 9th century, the Viking hordes began to swoop down on Britain, creating conflicts with the locals. The Anglo-Saxons would alternately fight, intermarry, and otherwise struggle with these Scandinavian newcomers.

As troubling as the Vikings could be, the Normans proved to be the greatest threat to Anglo-Saxon life. French-speaking tribes who hailed from Normandy, France, just across the English Channel, would come to control much of England. Led by

William the Conqueror in 1066, the Normans lorded over England for centuries until they were finally superseded by other forms of English nobility.

In the 1500s, the Tudor family took on prominence, with Henry VIII establishing his firm grip on English society. He even broke ties with the Catholic Church and put himself at the head of what would become the official Church of England. This began England's trend toward Protestantism and brought about a greater sense of nationalistic fervor.

The Glorious Revolution of 1688 served to ensure the precepts of the Magna Carta were followed to an even greater extent, further hammering out just how a king or queen of England should rule in Britain's constitutional monarchy. With these internal problems sorted out for a time, Britain would go on to rule the waves. Far-flung colonies would be established in both the Western and Eastern Hemispheres. The sun would not set on the British Empire for quite some time.

It was not until the end of World War Two that cracks began to emerge in the polished veneer of British imperialism. Imperial outposts in both the Middle East and Southeast Asia began to break away shortly after the war came to a close. India was torn loose in 1947, leading to much bloodshed and violence in the aftermath of its independence and subsequent partitioning, which rendered the modern-day state of Pakistan out of the northwest corner of the Indian subcontinent.

More global territorial changes were on the way, as the old dominions of Britain's previus empire began to crumble. All throughout the 1950s and 1960s, several African colonies vied for independence from Britain. As the decades wore on, the British Empire became smaller and smaller. Even so, when push came to shove, Britain proved it was still willing to fight for some of the leftover crumbs of extraterritorial domains that were still under its authority.

This was evidenced in the Falklands War, which took place in 1982. The Falkland Islands are a small group of otherwise obscure islets off the coast of Argentina. The Argentines wanted to claim the islands as their own, but once provoked by the threat of outright invasion, Britain laid down the hammer. British troops were deployed, and the islands were secured. The war still remains controversial, but Britain achieved its objectives, and the Falkland Islands remain part of the greatly diminished extraterritorial holdings of Britain.

Hong Kong was not quite so fortunate. According to an old agreement, Britain was forced to relinquish its Chinese territory back to mainland China. The handover still remains controversial since Hong Kong was one of the few former colonies of Britain that had a majority of the population wishing to remain under Britain's control. The people of Hong Kong had grown up with the democratic freedoms and capitalist economic policies of the West, and most had a hard time adjusting to being under the rule of communist China.

Britain would go through a variety of changes in the subsequent decades. In 2003, Britain partnered with the United States in the War on Terror, joining US forces in both Iraq and Afghanistan. British troops pulled out of Iraq in 2011, and ten years later, they were forced to pull out of Afghanistan.

The word "forced" must be used since the abrupt withdrawal of US troops under President Joe Biden largely seemed to catch Britain by surprise. Nevertheless, British operations in Afghanistan came to a close just in time for the British military to put its laser focus on the eruption of war in Ukraine in 2022—a conflict that is arguably more consequential than the war in Afghanistan had become.

Great Britain has since taken on a leading role in trying to find a solution to the ongoing crisis in Ukraine. As of this writing, no one is quite sure how all of these things might end. But one thing is for certain: the mighty island of Britain will most certainly play a part in it.

Here's another book by Captivating History that you might like

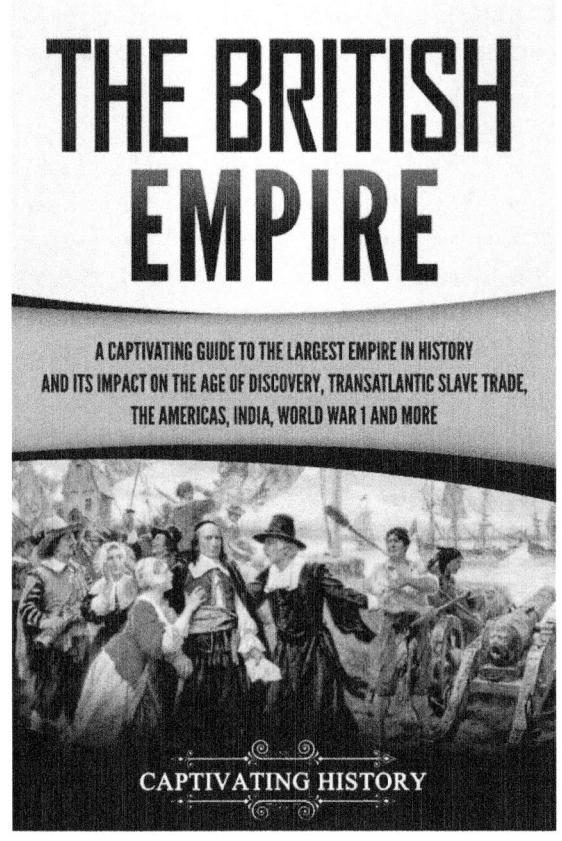

Free Bonus from Captivating History (Available for a Limited time)

Hi History Lovers!

Now you have a chance to join our exclusive history list so you can get your first history ebook for free as well as discounts and a potential to get more history books for free! Simply visit the link below to join.

Captivatinghistory.com/ebook

Also, make sure to follow us on Facebook, Twitter and Youtube by searching for Captivating History.

Appendix A: Further Reading and Reference

Dyer, Christopher. *Everyday Life in Medieval England*. 1994.

Hunter, Peter. *Roman Britain and Early England: 55 BC-871 AD*. 1966.

Levine, Philippa. *The British Empire: Sunrise to Sunset*. 2007.

McCourt, Malachy. *Malachy McCourt's History of Ireland*. 2001.

Schama, Simon. *A History of Britain*. 2000. (TV series)

Printed in Great Britain
by Amazon